21st CENTURY MANAGER

21st CENTURY MANAGER

MEETING THE CHALLENGES AND OPPORTUNITIES OF THE NEW CORPORATE AGE

GARETH S. GARDINER

PETERSON'S/PACESETTER BOOKS

PRINCETON, NEW JERSEY

21st Century Manager is published by Peterson's/Pacesetter Books.

Pacesetter Books, Peterson's Pacesetter Books, and the Pacesetter horse design are trademarks of Peterson's Guides, Inc.

Library of Congress Cataloging-in-Publication Data

Gardiner, Gareth.
    21st century manager : meeting the challenges and opportunities of the new corporate age / Gareth S. Gardiner.
    p. cm.
    Includes index.
    ISBN 1-56079-455-0
    1. Management—United States.   2. Management—Forecasting.   3. Twenty-first century—Forecasts.   I. Title.
    HD70.U5G37 1995
    658'.00973—dc20   95-18934
                                                                                        CIP

Editorial direction by Andrea Pedolsky   Creative direction by Linda Huber
Production supervision by Bernadette Boylan   Cover design by Kathy Kikkert
Proofreading by Marie Burnett   Cover illustration by Coco Masuda
Composition by Gary Rozmierski   Interior design by Cynthia Boone

Printed in the United States of America

10 9 8 7 6 5 4 3 2 1

Visit Peterson's Education & Career Center on the Internet (World Wide Web) at
http://www.petersons.com

ACKNOWLEDGMENTS

Many fine people are owed my heartiest thanks for their assistance in the preparation and publication of this book, but none more than Andrea Pedolsky of Peterson's, whose professional and conscientious editing has kept the project on track (and in focus) from the outset. Andrea is one of those proactive persons who sees opportunity and has all of the managerial skills that twenty-first-century managers will need in the facilitation of creative projects like this. Two good friends have also been most kind in taking time to read the manuscript and offer constructive suggestions at different stages of completion: Dr. Rick McKinney, of Edwardsville, Illinois; and Dr. Tom Minogue, of Champaign, Illinois.

Several of my graduate students have contributed useful and current publications that have greatly strengthened the book. Special notes of thanks are due Rob Lakritz of Nova Southeastern University, and Darlene Gallo, Jane Gausch, Nancy Nix-Rice, Vickie Newman, and Peggy Shaw of Lindenwood College. Jenifer Bridges has worked long and hard to input the manuscript as it has evolved and changed and has done it all on top of an already full schedule. My wife, Maureen, has been as patient as ever as I have labored to complete the book: my fits and starts are second nature to her, and her supportiveness has never wavered.

CONTENTS

INTRODUCTION

As the twenty-first century beckons, a truly global marketplace has arisen in which intense competition has forced business organizations in virtually every country on the planet to be leaner and more flexible: to meet the demands of customers as a matter of habit, to seek out new strategic opportunities, and to develop creative ways to maximize the inputs of the intelligent and entrepreneurial individuals associated with the new corporation. This is a book about how these goals can be achieved through management that is also lean and flexible, positive and proactive, and comfortable with the dynamic new diversity of the American (and global) workplace. I begin by examining the background of globalization and the pressures that have made the traditional, functional, hierarchical company dysfunctional. I also analyze the mind-sets that most of us have that block our creativity and force us into rigid and reactive patterns of conformity and stagnation.

The book develops a positive and proactive problem-solving model for twenty-first-century managers that virtually any man or woman of intelligence can use in a host of managerial situations. Proactive problem-solving skills can help us break out of habitual mind-sets and the pattern of rigidity that is their accompaniment and into a new world of freedom and flexibility. The opportunities are exciting for anyone willing to accept the challenge of change. Since humor is one important way we have of opening the windows of the mind, you should be warned that there are many attempts at levity and lightheartedness in these pages. Indeed, the book is often very "opunionated."

Twenty-First-Century Manager may well open some windows in your mind but only if you (as a consenting adult) let it. If you let it, it will focus your attention on why coaching and counseling skills are important in the twenty-first-century workplace; it will encourage you to consider that Management by Knowing When the Hell to Leave People Alone is sometimes a superior style; it will stimulate you to think about the rise of proactive and enlightened ethical choice in the new corporation, and it will share with you a vision of the future where employees are not only empowered decision-makers but *owners* of twenty-first-century companies. Most simply stated, I will challenge you to look forward and seize the opportunities that await proactive people in the new century. With any luck at all, you will also enjoy reading about these challenges and opportunities and expanding your managerial skills as the twenty-first century prepares to greet us all.

I

"THE OLD ORDER CHANGETH, YIELDING PLACE TO NEW"

Humpty Dumpty

Humpty Dumpty sat on a wall,
Humpty Dumpty had a great fall,
All the King's horses,
And all the King's men,
Couldn't put Humpty together again.

—Nursery rhyme, circa 1803

It's a done deal. The American corporation has been downsized, reengineered, and reinvented, and all in the space of about ten years. Beginning with AT&T and ending with Xerox, and with just about every alphabetic stop in between, virtually every major American firm has laid off a significant percentage of its permanent workforce. The layoffs began to attract attention in the mid to late 1980s and since that time have become an established phenomenon of the contemporary workplace. They have been accompanied, particularly in more recent years, by attempts to reorganize the companies carrying them out.

The unwanted and unwelcome layoffs have produced an uninvited but predictable psychological reaction: The traditional loyalty of employees to their corporate employers has been shattered and, like Humpty Dumpty, can never be put back together again. As the twenty-first century approaches, it has become clear that another organizational tradition has been shattered, also irreparably: The tradition of the company with a tall functional hierarchy, with bosses who give orders and workers who take them, with lots and lots of employees, and with each employee having one job. It once was a safe world, this traditional large corporation, and stable and prosperous. Millions of men and women spent their entire working lives with one company and then retired.

Humpty Dumpty Was Ready to Fall

In the blinding clarity of 20-20 hindsight, it is obvious why the major American corporation had to slim down, and fast. In a nation where well over half of the adult men and women (and about the same percentage of children) are overweight, the average big American company was also fat. Major corporations like General Motors and Ford had hundreds of thousands of employees and organizational hierarchies with as many as twenty different levels of decision-making authority. The organizational chart of a large American firm was a marvel of vertical elaboration and complexity.

The growth, and girth, of American companies was a direct result of the successful conclusion of World War II. The devastation of much of

Europe and Asia that was such an obvious and visible outcome of the war had a less obvious consequence: American industry was left unchallenged as the world leader. American firms had things their own way. In such basic industries as steel and automobile manufacturing, there was simply no significant foreign competition. What could be manufactured could be sold, both domestically and abroad, and the American economy boomed in the postwar years. Every major corporation enjoyed a period of sustained, unprecedented growth. American industry reached a zenith of prosperity and size.

And then the world changed (and changed and changed and changed). Beginning almost imperceptibly in the 1960s, as humble subcompact Japanese and German cars began to penetrate the domestic market; continuing in the 1970s, as the trickle of high-quality foreign imports became a flood; and reaching "crisis" proportions in the 1980s, as we became aware that big-league foreign competition was here to stay—the world became a single, global marketplace. And big American companies began to lose money, big money, for the first time in generations. Humpty Dumpty was ready to fall!

The facts of the matter are well-known. The big-three auto manufacturers were perhaps the most publicized big money losers, but historically profitable firms like U.S. Steel also hit the skids. Corporate name changes could not disguise the fact. The surest sign that the apocalypse was upon us was when IBM—Big Blue—went from blue-chip winner to stunned money loser in an amazingly short stretch of time in the early 1990s.

Crisis management has always been the forte of the American nation (unfortunately, excellent management of crises is usually necessitated by poor anticipation and planning). When we are taken unawares and lose the battle, as we did at Pearl Harbor, we recover smartly and win the war. It is precisely the crisis that gets us going and leads to the development of such awful clichés as "When the going gets tough, the tough get going." Let us all groan together.

In any event, American business began to suffer a real crisis of confidence in the mid 1980s in the face of stiffening global competition, and corporate downsizing was a predictable reaction to the recognition that American companies were fat, not very happy, and increasingly unprofitable. In a real way, layoffs became something of yet another quick fix for a problem with long-term causes: Lay off a bunch of people, and lay them off fast. In most cases something had to be done, and quickly, but it was the *manner* of the downsizing, particularly in the early years, that led to the changing face of employee motivation, loyalty, and morale.

It is perhaps ironic that the very method chosen to cut business costs quickly and make the company more competitive often failed to accomplish that, even in the short run. Writing in *Time* magazine, in an article entitled "When Downsizing Becomes 'Dumbsizing' " Bernard Baumhol remarked that ". . . there is mounting evidence that this slash-and-burn labor policy is backfiring. Studies now show that a number of companies that trimmed their workforces not only failed to see a rebound in earnings but found their ability to compete eroded even further."[1] Companies that had laid off workers in an arbitrary manner continued to encounter serious productivity problems—one of the main reasons was the bitter unhappiness of employees left behind.

After six million layoffs between 1987 and 1992, involving hundreds of firms, the American Management Association surveyed some five hundred companies that had made major reductions. The results? Three quarters had suffered serious reductions in employee morale. Two thirds showed no increase in productivity. Fewer than half enjoyed increased profits.[2] In analyzing these negative results, a clear and distinct pattern of poor management emerges.

Some Really Dumb Ways of Downsizing

When American philosopher George Santayana remarked that those who cannot remember the past are condemned to repeat it, he obviously did not have the major American corporations of the late twentieth century in mind. But he might as well have. It is absolutely extraordinary, in studying the first waves of layoffs, how ill-considered and poorly handled most of them were. Small wonder that employees left behind were often bitter, defensive, and unproductive.

The layoffs that were badly handled, or bungled, had some common characteristics, all of them typical of a managerial mind-set more associated with the nineteenth century than the latter part of the twentieth:

1. *Announce major layoffs after reporting a highly profitable year.* Layoffs that are announced in the midst of profitability and rising sales guarantee an immediate surge of anger and resentment.

Employees at all levels in every organization have come to expect increased rewards in periods of prosperity: This is an expectation that transcends the entire history of industrial (and preindustrial) societies. Management can add insult to injury in this regard by making a pious pronouncement that while present profits are good, major problems of productivity and competitiveness lie just ahead unless the workforce is reduced significantly. Whatever the truth of such a prediction, it is immediately perceived by employees as a self-serving and transparent lie. And in downsizing situations, as in most of life, perception is reality: Management has shot itself right in the foot.

2. *Give no prior warning of layoffs.* In the 1950s and 1960s Douglas McGregor of Harvard University became famous for popularizing the notion that if management has "Theory X" assumptions about the workforce (assumes that workers are lazy and shiftless, to put it most simply), it will consistently engage in actions that bring about a self-fulfilling prophecy.[3] In the case of downsizing layoffs, management fears that its untrustworthy workforce will react with intense anger to being downsized, so it engages in an attempt to hide or disguise the layoffs. The futility of this in the electronic age hardly needs to be mentioned: Management's attempts at secrecy immediately lead to an explosion of information and misinformation in the organizational grapevine, and an attack of paranoia sweeps through the firm. (One of the most pernicious effects of paranoia, unfortunately, is that it infects just about everyone.) Everyone becomes fearful and suspicious, productivity suffers, worker loyalty goes into the tank, and the entire company becomes suffused with anger. Management, as is the case with any neurotic anxiety, has brought about exactly what it fears. When the dreaded layoff finally occurs in such a wretched and hostile environment, locks *must* be changed, employees *must* be escorted off the premises by armed security personnel, and the company's legal department *must* be alerted to an impending onslaught of lawsuits.

3. *Provide little or no severance pay and benefits.* Most, if not all, companies that are downsizing offer outgoing employees *some* kind of severance package, usually based on years of service. There is so much variance among these packages that it is difficult to characterize them adequately in a sentence or two,* but they all have to pass a litmus test: Are they fair? In a psychologically painful situation, where an employee already feels abused, the perception of fairness will obviously be somewhat precarious. A very simple and fair statement can be made in this connection: When a long-term outgoing employee is offered a severance package that he or she sees as a miserable pittance, trouble is bound to follow.

One of my former students, now a senior human resource executive at a large company in St. Louis, worked for a company in the late 1980s that decided to downsize. Her unhappy responsibility

---

* The reader will immediately note that I cheerfully cop out in the face of such daunting challenges.

was to inform each employee, one at a time, of the decision, and explain the severance package during the same interview. While this particular company offered terminated employees a relatively generous package, the general reaction to it was, not surprisingly, negative. In reaction to his proposed settlement, one employee made the memorable remark that the company was not only "uncaring and inhuman" but "awfully Goddamn cheap."[4] In the most litigious society on earth, such an unfortunate linkage of perceptions often leads (naturally) to lengthy and expensive litigation, even when employees sign a written agreement promising not to sue.

4. *Tell the world that the layoffs have to be made because "everyone's doing it."* It is widely believed by intelligent people that companies downsize because they have developed an ingenious master plan to reorganize and restructure the business—a plan so carefully thought out that the success of the organization is guaranteed for generations to come. Not! And particularly in the early years of the phenomenon. In many cases, the layoffs were the product of management by conformity, a widely used management methodology that appears in none of the scholarly textbooks. The name adequately describes the technique: Do exactly what you see the management of similar or competing firms doing.

Management consultant A. Gary Shilling, remarking on this problem, noted that "there is tremendous peer pressure to get rid of workers. Everybody is doing it because they think they have to."[5] Conformity, and excessive conformity, is a fact of American life that psychologists and sociologists have been decrying for some two generations now, and it is probably not surprising that it is just as pervasive in business decision making as it is in social life. Most executives are not so naive or tactless as to make a public announcement that they have laid off five hundred workers because the ABC company just did the same. Instead, the press release making the fact public is couched in a careful kind of corporate doublespeak: "XYZ company, in response to competitive pressures within the widget industry, regretfully announced today that it will be laying off five hundred production and middle-management personnel within the next eight weeks. A generous severance package will be offered to all affected employees." Rarely, in the real world, do the authors of doublespeak get straight, honest, and direct feedback about its impact; namely, that almost everyone reading it or hearing it perceives it immediately as doublespeak. Many affected persons rapidly replace "doublespeak" with less discreet euphemisms or expressions, which are left to the rich imagination of the reader.

5. *Make the layoffs virtually at random.* Another widely used management methodology not appearing in the traditional management textbooks is MBCCP—Management by Crisis, Chaos, and Panic. The early pattern of layoffs that appeared when downsizing became a phenomenon exemplified many of the characteristics of MBCCP: wild and random hacking away at groups of employees; hysterical pronouncements of impending doom, or at least bankruptcy; a good deal of lying about the company's true intentions; and rather silly statements about the situation being totally under control. One can easily exaggerate some of these managerial actions, but many of them were quite clearly taken in a virtual state of panic and were accurately perceived as being made in such a state.

Random, slash-and-burn layoffs fooled neither employees, management analysts, nor the stock market. Executives who expected their company's stock price to dramatically soar after a hasty downsizing were often sorely disappointed (bad pun intended): The price sagged after Wall Street gurus could discern no coherent strategy in the layoffs and said so. Layoffs for the sake of layoffs were perceived neither as a panacea nor even a quick fix by financial markets, which are usually not fooled by cosmetic (if wrenching) changes.

From Downsizing to Reengineering: Closing Out the Twentieth Century

The American nation is not always admired internationally for its virtual addiction to quick-fix solutions for a host of societal and management problems, but it *is* admired for its ability to develop quick and snappy labels and catchy acronyms for both new approaches to dealing with problems and for problems that are eternal. Who can forget, for example, the World War II acronyms that developed to describe bureaucratic snags that have plagued every military operation since the days of Alexander the Great: SNAFU (loosely translated as situation normal, all fouled up) and FUBAR (fouled up beyond all reason)?

While the downsizing movement has not yet produced acronyms to rival these two, it *has* produced terms that have become buzzwords in discussions of changes in the modern workplace. The first such buzzword was, of course, downsizing. Downsizing resulted in the "lean and mean" organization, a term that has already achieved cliché status, and in record time. As the human costs of downsizing become more and more apparent, including lengthening work weeks for survivors (in manufacturing the average work week had increased to nearly 42 hours by the summer of 1993, the longest in nearly 30 years), those observers of management who are more cynical or skeptical than most began to suggest that the lean-and-mean organization was probably just plain mean.

Buzzwords often have an important and creative function that transcends mere "cuteness." They lead serious students of change to begin dealing with the problems that the acronyms and labels describe so deftly and briefly. As it became more obvious that the downsized organization was often just a plain "downer," with declining morale and profitability, the search began for a methodology or technique for restructuring companies that would enhance their competitiveness in a world increasingly gone global without the nasty side-effects of an arbitrary and brutal downsizing. Thus was the reengineering, or reinvention, movement born.*

---

* I unhesitatingly and daringly make great historical leaps that may defy conventional wisdom or logic.

A pioneering effort in the field was *Re-Inventing the Corporation*, a 1985 book by John Naisbitt and Patricia Aburdene.[6] Aside from their early use of the term "reinvention," which referred to making work more interesting and meaningful, these authors talked about "throwing out the organization chart," decentralizing authority, eliminating a host of "perks" and other trappings of formal authority, and in general infusing the organization with humanistic values. They also introduced themes that will be returned to in this book: The true role of the manager is teacher and coach, the top-down management style has become obsolete, quality is a major key to success, large corporations must emulate the entrepreneurial style of smaller businesses, and employees must be given a new and much higher degree of autonomy.

While Tom Peters and Bob Waterman had visited some of the same territory in their 1982 classic *In Search of Excellence*[7] (excellent firms like Wal-Mart and McDonald's are driven by values, are customer-oriented, value employee risk-taking and entrepreneurship, keep the form of the organization simple, and believe in the wisdom of the great American acronym KISS—keep it simple, stupid!), Naisbitt and Aburdene were among the first management scholars to recognize a new reality: The classical, vertical organizational hierarchy had in many ways become a dinosaur. Our traditional way of organizing and structuring the corporation was becoming increasingly dysfunctional in a global age, with tremendous competitive pressures coming to bear on companies— pressures totally undreamed of only a few years earlier.

A flood of literature began to pour forth, and the reengineering wave became a virtual tsunami in the late 1980s and early 1990s. Authors differed somewhat in their approaches and emphases, but this sea change in organizational thinking and philosophy had common themes. The first of these, another indigenous American label, was the emergence of the "horizontal corporation."

The first trickle of downsizing had been almost random, but when the trickle became an open spigot, the individuals most likely to be flushed out were the men and women who were middle managers. Corporations cut out layers of middle management because they realized they simply had too many vertical levels in their organizations, which led to familiar (and bureaucratic) problems in communication and efficiency: slowness, distortion, SNAFUs, and even *gridlock* (another American label originally developed to describe endless delays on the nation's freeways—a true oxymoron of a name). The fact that the individuals filling middle-level positions were also very well compensated became another incentive for downsizing: Costs could be quickly and visibly cut by slimming the ranks of middle management.

Many companies found that when their production workers were without such hands-on supervision, their productivity actually increased. When the impact of layoffs fell most heavily on workers, however, the opposite often occurred: productivity declined. Top management in this country has often been accused of myopia; but in this case, even a blind pig had found an acorn, if an old expression can be adapted creatively.

The new horizontal corporation can be characterized by several features. First among them is the organization of work around process, not task. This insight, which recognizes that every corporation has *core processes* that add value to it, such as manufacturing or sales, has led to a dramatic move away from the dominance of functional departments, such as corporate accounting or engineering, which were preeminent in the vertical hierarchy.

When a company is organized around core work processes, functional departments no longer get in the way of getting the work done. Department heads are replaced by team leaders. Work teams that manage key work processes are largely self-managing, since every member and the team itself are accountable for getting the job done. Autonomous and empowered work teams thus are a second feature of the horizontal organization.

A third feature was derived from the exploding total quality management (TQM) movement. The organization must be customer driven: Customer satisfaction becomes the major motivation of the entire company, on the assumption that the traditional bottom line (profitability and a rising stock price) will follow in time, if not immediately. Customer satisfaction as a prime motivator is accompanied by the organizational need to bring all employees into regular and continuing contact with its suppliers and customers. The vertical organization, unfortunately, interacts largely with itself, and interaction with customers is extremely irregular, except in the sales departments and customer service organizations.

The organization that uses teams of empowered individuals to accomplish most of the work must reward their performance. Since work teams in the horizontal corporation typically have broad, not narrow, work assignments requiring versatility, flexibility, and multiple skills, the reward structure must be changed to reflect that fact, and career development or progression must be considered in a whole new light—the fourth feature of the horizontal organization. The concept of the career corporate ladder climber has been the first to disappear under a rock in this bright new world, and the conventional concept of what constitutes a successful career in the world of organizations is also being revised.

In a cover story on the emergence of the horizontal corporation, *Business Week* staff writer John Byrne cited AT&T, Eastman Chemical, General Electric, Motorola, and Xerox as major companies already making extensive use of horizontal design features.[8] In such organizations, senior managers must have "multiple competencies" rather than narrow specializations in order to be able to effectively coordinate people and processes. He emphasized, also, that employees need to be trained not in specializations but in how to handle and process information intelligently, how to make their own decisions, and how to become more autonomous and self-directing in all their organizational activities.

Byrne's article is particularly interesting because it contains a compelling graphic displaying organizational charts, or at least organizational models, for the modern horizontal corporation (see page 18). Gone is the traditional box-and-line hierarchy, still displayed prominently and frequently in introductory management texts; arrived is a series of creative, and even fanciful, representations of what the new corporate models might look like. The Eastman Chemical pizza chart, so-called because it resembles a pepperoni pizza, is drawn in a circular form to indicate that everyone is equal in the organization. Pepsi's inverted pyramid puts field reps at the top to illustrate its focus on

Some Models of the Horizontal Organization

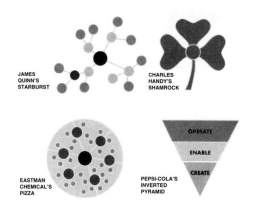

From John Byrne, "The Horizontal Corporation," *Business Week*, December 20, 1993, pp. 80–81. Reprinted with permission.

customers; Charles Handy, a lecturer at the London Business School, drew a shamrock figure to represent the combined force of employees, contractors, and part-timers; while James Quinn of Dartmouth College created a starburst to show a company splitting off units like shooting stars. Writer Byrne stresses that these cheerful creations are merely early approximations of the final form of the horizontal organizations, because ". . . it's simply too early."

It may indeed be early, but these graphical representations of emerging forms of organization are more than merely another example of our American ability to capture new ideas in a catchy way (with a deserved bow to a creative Brit in the group): They demonstrate dramatically and visually how *flexible* the horizontal corporation is relative to the vertical hierarchy. The accelerating pace of change in the modern world, decried by many but recognized by all, is the great engine driving the transformational changes taking place all over the globe.

While the rigid (even in appearance) traditional "tall" organization is not well equipped to cope with change because it must expend so much energy dealing with the bureaucratic barriers within itself, the horizontal or "flat" organization is fluid and flexible in form and function, is relatively unencumbered by internal constraints, and has energy left over to deal with a world that goes right on changing. It can develop new products quickly and efficiently. It can utilize human ability and creativity. And it can satisfy the demand of a global marketplace that products and services meet the continuing imperative of quality.

The Quality Imperative in a Global Community

During the fat-and-happy period enjoyed by American industry after World War II, a quiet and virtually unnoticed movement began in Japan, aided and abetted by expatriate Americans. As Japanese industry rebuilt its shattered infrastructure after the devastation wreaked by the war, it faced a daunting competitive challenge; namely, the American behemoth. As a resource-starved nation that had to export to survive, Japan realized early that it must embrace quality in a brave new world.

The resulting success story has of course become a legend. At the invitation of (the legendary) General Douglas MacArthur, Dr. W. Edwards Deming was invited to Japan, initially as an adviser to the Japanese census. His preachments on quality and quality control found a receptive audience in Japan, particularly among top executives who accepted Deming's repeated offers to meet directly with them. No blind pigs, these executives: They rapidly spotted the acorn. As early as the 1950s at major corporations like Toyota, Deming's ideas were already being implemented.

Deming was a prophet without honor in his own land, while becoming a guru in Japan. American executives, who had not yet spied the acorn, were simply not interested in listening to his ideas. It is interesting and instructive, however, that first-line managers and production workers in Deming's homeland were enthusiastic about the ideas that were to become the basis of the quality revolution: building quality into products rather than inspecting it out; full participation by employees in the quality process, including implementing their suggestions for improvement; heavy emphasis on on-the-job training to facilitate improvement; breaking down organizational barriers between groups and departments; driving out fear, so that everyone in the company works effectively; and, above all, recognizing that the customer is King—and Queen.*

By the mid 1970s the American consumer had clearly recognized the superior quality of Japanese products, particularly Japanese automobiles, and the rush was on. By 1978 Ford Motor Company executives learned of Deming's ideas while on a visit to Japan and extended him an

---

* It is ironic that while the Japanese were quick to recognize the value of the quality movement, they have been very slow to recognize the value of including women at every level in the contemporary business organization, a blind spot that (while slowly being removed) will continue to damage their competitiveness well into the twenty-first century.

invitation to work with Ford. By 1981 he was hard at work in Dearborn, which may have caused Henry Ford to turn in his grave, but Ford's early association with Deming was a major cause of the company's highly successful turnaround and its rapidly growing reputation in the 1980s and 1990s as a model of quality in the automobile industry.

The total quality management, or TQM, movement swept through the world in the 1980s and 1990s. Americans have always cherished gurus and prophets, and during this era Deming, Joseph M. Juran, and Philip Crosby all achieved hallowed status. As the world economy continued to become more global, driven by advanced communications and computer technology, a healthy form of conformity and competition thrived: Quality became a precondition for competing in the global economy.[9]

Unlike some of the management fads that took hold in American industry in previous generations—such as Management by Objectives (MBO) in the 1960s and the first wave of downsizing in the 1980s—the TQM movement did not promise yet another quick fix for industry's problems. Indeed, its philosophy of continuous improvement was a sobering reminder to management and workers alike that a commitment to quality was going to be both long-term and continuing. Even though literally millions of words have been written about the history and practice of TQM, its impact on the workplace and on management practices and skills has not always been fully understood. Along with the other powerful change forces described in these pages, TQM has transformed organizations and management in three ways, all of which are interrelated:

1. It has forced corporations to become more democratic, decentralized and participative—employees are not only *listened to* at every level, but they are fully involved in day-to-day decision making and strategy formation.

2. It has required that *fear* be driven out of the organization, particularly among employees, so that the entire organization can become more creative and willing to take risks.

3. It has stressed that employees must be *empowered*, with real authority to make decisions and to take entrepreneurial risks.

The Demise of Bureaucracy and the Rise of Entrepreneurship

In the clarity of hindsight, if a metaphor may be continued, it is not too surprising that communist economies throughout the world collapsed in the late 1980s and 1990s. In the great fog bank of foresight, however, it is still amazing. As the break-up of the former Soviet Union effectively ended the Cold War, and as the eastern European states democratized and returned to private enterprise, and as mainland China developed an exploding free market within the framework of an increasingly unworkable authoritarian government, observers everywhere continued to ask, "What happened?"

The answer is simply that the demise of the communist system has been part of a global pattern of change: the decline, everywhere, of bureaucratic vertical organizations and the rise of entrepreneurial, democratic, and decentralized organizations, countries, and corporations.

The huge central bureaucracies that developed to run the command economies of the authoritarian communist states were simply not working. The communist nations everywhere were dirt poor, consumers had almost no choice of goods, the quality of life was uniformly shabby, and everyone knew it. Because of global communications it had become increasingly difficult, if not impossible, for governments to deny information to citizens about the changes occurring around the world: The citizens of the communist states knew as well as the rest of us that they were getting a bad deal.

It is both fitting and ironic that the arrival of the information age has produced the very opposite of the result envisioned by George Orwell when he wrote *1984*.[10] Satellite-based communications, VCRs, cellular telephones, high-powered personal computers, the Internet, and transworld communications of every sort have given the individual more power, not less. In every advanced nation, and in many developing ones, authoritarian governments with their accompanying bureaucracies* have run into trouble. The denial of economic choice, which lies at the heart of every authoritarian government and command economy, thus becomes more and more unachievable. Individuals everywhere are empowered by the new technology, and empowered individuals demand a piece of the action.

The rise of entrepreneurship all over the world, and its resurgence in the United States, with accompanying values of self-reliance, achieve-

---

* A bureaucracy is any organization, public or private, that does not have to submit itself to the discipline of the marketplace.

ment motivation, and independent thinking, has been a direct outcome of the information age and the global economy. Russian entrepreneurs are beginning to transform a moribund economy, admittedly with many bumps along the way. Chinese entrepreneurs thrive despite the lingering vestiges of a communist government. American entrepreneurs continue to lead the world in vigor and creativity. The new wave of entrepreneurs around the world, and in this country, presents a new challenge and an exciting new opportunity to the twenty-first-century organization.

New Forms of Loyalty in the Workplace: Twenty-First-Century Management

Lester Digman of the University of Nebraska–Lincoln is a distinguished scholar in the field of strategic management,[11] but one of the most memorable phrases in his many books and articles is this truism: "In every threat there is an opportunity, and in every opportunity, a threat." While Digman probably had the strategic choices faced by companies in mind when he penned these words of wisdom, they apply equally well to the changes that are taking place in the American workplace. The new generation of employees arriving through corporate doors is a clear threat to traditional top-down, authoritarian management practices, which assume that employees will be slavishly loyal and unendingly faithful to the employer, no matter how they are treated. The world has changed, and the twenty-first century beckons.

For twenty-first-century management, a new opportunity presents itself: the opportunity to *earn* the loyalty of employees by offering them exciting, sometimes entrepreneurial, chances for personal growth and empowerment in organizations that are free, flat, fair, and flexible. *Free* organizations compete in free markets and face the sometimes stern discipline of the marketplace; *flat* organizations have cut out unnecessary layers of management, reengineered, and minimized internal bureaucracy; *fair* organizations realize that a new generation of employees will respond best to management practices that are up front, equitable, ethical, and honest; *flexible* organizations are customer-driven, forward-looking, and quick to respond to the changing demands of people, technology, and the marketplace. The challenges faced by twenty-first century managers in such a dynamic organizational environment will require a new managerial mind-set, problem-solving skills, leadership style, and philosophy of management. It is truly the dawning of a new managerial age.

NINETEENTH-CENTURY-MANAGEMENT REVISITED

In Praise of Bureaucrats (Well, sort of)

Beginning with Richard Nixon, six consecutive U.S. Presidents have attempted to downsize the most sacred temple of contemporary bureaucracy, the American federal government. This has produced blips on the radar screen from time to time, but otherwise the picture has been steady: The growth of the federal bureaucracy continues, virtually unabated. Controlling the federal government has long since ceased to be a partisan issue: Politicians of every persuasion and generation literally foam at the mouth when the immense size and power of our federal establishment is the subject of conversation (or the focus of desperation).

Many highly intelligent analysts have asked why it is that the bureaucrats outlast even the most determined elected officials. Part of the answer, obviously, is that elected officials are in office for a term or two—or twelve, in the case of some congressmen and women—but bureaucrats are in office forever. New federal administrations typically replace the men and women at the top of a tall pyramid or agency, but all those persons underneath stay, and seemingly for eternity.

Another part of the answer, equally obvious, is that the bureaucrats are not subject to the discipline of the marketplace—they do not need to make a buck. They are not accountable to the powerful forces that have transformed private organizations throughout the world—or at least not accountable yet. Even the most dramatically bungled operation—such as the federal raid on the Branch Davidian compound near Waco, Texas, in

1993—normally results in only the most mild disciplinary action extending to a very few miscreants. The offending agency does not go broke, and life goes on pretty much as usual after the media flurry subsides.

While the apocalypse may yet be coming, probably in the form of privatization of *many* government functions, the capacity of bureaucrats to survive is simply astonishing, and no accident. Over the decades— indeed, centuries—bureaucrats have honed skills that have allowed them to endure, while the Sphinx has crumbled. These survival skills, while well-known in bureaucratic culture, are not equally well understood among the general population. The time has truly come for them to be enshrined (in a suitable temple, on appropriate legal tablets) for all the world to see.

The survival credo of the generic bureaucrat is embodied in the following statements, which eschew obfuscation and defy all attempts at rational analysis:

1. "I'd like to help but I can't do that because it's not in my job description." This statement demonstrates a true desire to help, but, alas, the job description carved in granite precludes any action. So sorry.

2. "I've referred your request to a higher level of authority." Again, I'm trying to be helpful as hell, but those higher authorities need to take action on such an important request. Just try to find the higher level of authority, however. I dare you.

3. "We can do that, but I'm going to need several more staff members, and a new budget, to get it done." The private sector measures

success in profits and losses, the bureaucrat by how many staff members he has and how big his empire has become. Every request to do something represents an opportunity to expand the empire. Dynasty time!

4. "Your problem is under very careful review, I can assure you." Helpful as hell, as always, but he doesn't add that the damned review is going to take twenty-two years.

5. "We have to evaluate that request in view of the mission and goals of the agency." Trying to define our mission is truly going to be a challenge, and we already know how long the evaluation is going to take (see #4).

6. "I'm so busy, busy, busy right now that it's going to be a while before I can get to it." A generation ago, C. Northcote Parkinson enunciated his most famous law of bureaucracy—that work expands so as to fill the time available to do it. Every bureaucrat knows this deep in his or her soul. Business (excuse: busy-ness) is the essence of survival. Keep busy, and keep employed. Take a 15-minute task and make it last 30. Take a one-hour job and make it a last day. Where there's a will, there's a way.

Years ago Alfred, Lord Tennyson, penned the famous line, "The old order changeth, yielding place to new." In this case, the old order changeth, to be sure, but the change is mighty slow.

TWENTY-FIRST-CENTURY MANAGEMENT IN ACTION

What Makes Plants More Flexible? It's the People, Of Course!

The arrival of the computer in American industry brought with it the promise of a miracle. Wide-scale use of computers, it was assumed, would make factories more productive, more efficient, and more flexible. High levels of computer integration in any one plant, further, would almost certainly give that facility a big edge on less integrated competitors. In the late twentieth century, manufacturing managers began focusing on the *flexibility* of a plant (meaning its ability to fill customer orders quickly and introduce new products easily) as a variable critical to success. In industry after industry, strong competition in nearly every area, but most notably in cost and quality, made it clear that flexibility would be increasingly important in the new century.

In a different type of paper chase, Harvard Business School professor David M. Upton set out to determine why the achievement of flexibility has been so difficult in so many industries. The targets of his research were sixty-one paper factories located all over North America, which were chosen for the study because they all made very similar products. Since different types of paper differ from each other only in fairly basic ways—such as weight—Upton reasoned that it would be fairly easy for him to measure the differences in flexibility among the plants.

First and foremost, Upton discovered that the degree of computer integration in the paper plants simply did not matter. "My findings turn much of the conventional wisdom on its head. In the plants I studied there was little direct correlation between the degree of computer integration and the degree of operational flexibility."[12] He also found that the size of the plant did not influence flexibility and that a more experienced workforce was sometimes an impediment. What *did* matter, in plant after plant, was its management. In plants where management made flexibility a high priority and communicated this clearly to the workers, there was greater flexibility.

Interestingly, even the most sophisticated computer-integration systems did not decrease time needed to switch from making one product to making another. In many of the plants, teams of operators were much faster than the computer in changing the plant over and took great pride in this fact. One reason for their success was that they were able to avoid catastrophic failures, such as paper breaks, that could consume great chunks of changeover time. Another was that they found creative, if risky, techniques to outperform the computer.

In discussing ways that manufacturing managers can make their operations more flexible, Upton first stresses the importance of deciding what type of flexibility they want and how it can be measured. He then mentions the importance of training to build flexibility: to get workers beyond a "this is the way we've always done it" mind-set and to build their confidence. Third, he notes that training also helps build esprit de corps and a sense of community. But practice makes perfect, as the saying goes, and he concludes that flexibility can be improved by *practicing* it. People and good management make even more of a difference, it seems, in a highly technical age.

ENDNOTES

1. Bernard Baumhol, "When Downsizing Becomes 'Dumbsizing,' " *Time*, March 5, 1993, p. 55.

2. Baumhol, p. 55.

3. Douglas McGregor, *The Human Side of Enterprise* (New York: McGraw-Hill, 1960).

4. Personal communication to the author, September 15, 1994.

5. Baumhol, p. 55.

6. John Naisbitt and Patricia Aburdene, *Re-Inventing the Corporation* (New York: Warner Books, 1985).

7. Thomas Peters and Robert Waterman Jr., *In Search of Excellence* (New York: Harper & Row, 1982).

8. John Byrne, "The Horizontal Corporation," *Business Week*, December 20, 1993, pp. 76–81.

9. Robert Gatewood, Robert Taylor, and O. C. Ferrell, *Management: Comprehension, Analysis, and Application* (Homewood, IL: The Austen Press, 1995).

10. George Orwell, *1984* (New York: Signet Classics, 1950).

11. Lester Digman, *Strategic Management*, 2nd ed. (Homewood, IL: BPI Irwin, 1990).

12. David M. Upton, "What Really Makes Factories Flexible?" *Harvard Business Review* (July–August 1995): pp. 74–84.

2

BREAKING MANAGERIAL MIND-SETS AND INCREASING MANAGERIAL FLEXIBILITY

"Just Another Emotional Woman"

Jean Smith was a training director at a Midwestern regional office of the United States Office of Personnel Management (OPM). One afternoon after I had completed a daylong training session dealing with prejudice and rigid thinking, we sat down together and she related the following experience she had recently had at OPM:

"You know, Gary, your class today reminded me of something that happened here at work the other day. I've always suspected that my boss, Bill Roberts, is prejudiced against women, particularly in professional positions like mine, but this incident confirmed it. He's made a number of remarks in the three years I've been here about women being extremely emotional and undependable, and even though I won the outstanding employee award last year, I was still the target for a few of these remarks.

Well, a couple of weeks ago my car broke down in a snowstorm on the way to work, two of my kids were sick with the flu and my regular baby-sitter wouldn't take them, my ex-husband made an abusive telephone call just before I left the house, and the worst sinus infection I've ever had was dragging me down. When I finally got to work, 30 minutes late—the first time I've been late in three years—Bill immediately came into my office and demanded to know why I had come in late. It was the final straw, and I just couldn't help it—I broke down and cried. And do you know what Bill Roberts said? He said, 'See, this proves it, I knew you were just another emotional woman.'"

A year later, Jean Smith left OPM for a position with a private employer as a senior vice president in human resource management.*

Very few things are more disturbing to the average person of good sense and good will than the idea that he or she is prejudiced. Insult is added to injury if it is suggested that in addition to being prejudiced, he or she is also rigid and inflexible and the victim of habitual mind-sets that can create major problems in the management of people, change, and problems. In an important way, our feeling of goodness, and our sense of self-esteem, is bound up in our concept of ourselves as fair-minded, decent, and honorable. And most of us *are* these things, of course: basically decent, fair, and honorable. Most of us are pretty normal, in a society that values normalcy.

* As usual, all names, dates, and places have been changed to protect the innocent, the guilty, and the unconscious.

Yet the very mental processes we use that make us normal (and sane, and smart!) can create serious hazards for us in situations requiring a different type of thinking and an ability to cope with problems of change in a flexible, proactive, and creative way. Bill Roberts is probably no better or worse than most of us, would be shocked and offended if told that he thinks like a sexist pig, and probably is amazed that he has management problems with women and other employees. After two centuries, the well-worn words of Scottish poet Robbie Burns still ring in our ears:

> "Oh wad some power the giftie gie us
> To see oursels as ithers see us!"[1]

For the twenty-first-century manager, it is precisely the ability to be flexible and proactive, and to stay solidly in touch with reality, that will prove to be the key to managerial success.

Some Normal Habits of Thought That Serve Us Well

A friendly instructor holds up a familiar round paper object in front of a graduate business class in organizational behavior. "What is this object that I'm holding up in front of you, class?" he asks innocently. "Quickly, please, tell me what it is." The ever alert and suspicious class, wise to their instructor's crafty and devious ways, pauses for only a moment, and then confidently replies, "It's a coffee cup. It's a paper cup. You're drinking coffee from it. Anyone can see it's a paper cup." The instructor pauses dramatically, and intones, "Well of course it is, class. Anyone can see it's a paper cup. But come on now, tell me what else it is."

The class pauses for a moment. There are signs of reflection among most of its members, silence being the principal indicator. In a few seconds, a chorus of voices begins. "It's a soda cup." "It's a pencil holder." "Its general use is as a container—it could contain all kinds of things." The container uses for the familiar object now being well established, more exotic uses are rapidly offered up. "It could be used as building material." "Put a string through it, and it could be part of a two-way radio." "Cut it open and spread it out, and you could use it as a writing pad in an emergency." Within minutes, dozens of uses for the familiar paper cup are suggested by the class.

"Why did I ask you to do this?" the instructor now wants to know. "Because it took up five minutes of class time, sir," announces the first voice, that of the class humorist. A discussion follows, and some normal habits of mind that bright people use everywhere in solving problems are identified. First is the ability to identify familiar objects quickly and accurately. An ability that is universally shared among intelligent adults in all cultures is recognizing familiar shapes and forms without hesitation or doubt. When the question is asked, "Did you ever have any *doubt* that it was a coffee cup?" there are bemused looks throughout the group.

The point is now made that we normally are very confident of the rightness and correctness of the thousands of judgments that we make about familiar objects each day. We are used to being right, because we usually *are* right. If we had to stop and think each time we approached a stop sign or stooped down to tie our shoes, we would of course be spending most of our time on routine judgments and decisions that we make habitually and instantaneously. The mental ability adults have to do this is one of the things that makes us smart and has helped the species survive.

Our routine judgments are also a daily reassurance that we are in fact *sane*: that we see the world the way it is, that we are not hallucinating while we are on the job (although the average American daydreams for up to two hours during a typical day's work), that we are normal people (how reassuring that *everyone* in the graduate class in business sees the familiar object as a coffee cup), and that generally speaking we are competent people. When the members of the class are asked if they are sane, the question rapidly becomes a creative and humorous vehicle of conversation, but it also makes a serious point: We need to have confidence in our sanity and intelligence as we conduct our daily business.

The Mind-Sets That Make Us Smart Make Us Stupid

Mind-sets may be defined quite simply as habits of mind: automatic ways of perceiving and thinking about the world. Mind-sets also *predispose* us to see or think about people and events in certain ways. The perceptive reader will notice the similarity between the words predispose and prejudge. When I show a group of sane and smart and sober adult students in my business seminars the ambiguous drawing that

The Old Woman/Young Woman Picture

appears here and ask, "What is this a picture of?" those who have not seen the picture previously will give one of two different replies. "It's an old woman," say some. "Boy is she ugly!" or "It's a young woman." "She's dressed like she might be going out for the evening." All the members of the seminar see either the picture of the young woman *or* the old woman within a split second, but no one sees both pictures simultaneously. Indeed, most people who see one image often have difficulty seeing the other.

Many years ago psychologist Robert Leeper[2] played an interesting game with the old woman/young woman picture, which takes advantage of normal habits of mind that we all have. He first showed his subjects either a drawing of the young woman or the old woman, but the drawing was done so that the image was clear and strong and not ambiguous. He then showed them the ambiguous picture you have just been looking at. All of the people who were originally exposed to the first picture of the old woman said that they saw the old woman in the ambiguous picture, and 95 percent shown the picture of the young woman first said that they saw her in the ambiguous picture.

A variation of this experiment is sometimes conducted in psychology classes studying perception. The old woman/young woman drawing is arranged as a series of twenty pictures or slides. In the first slide the image of the old woman is very strong and the young woman almost invisible. When the student viewers are asked "What is this a picture of?" almost all of them will say, "It's an old woman."

As each slide is shown, the image of the old woman begins to recede, and the picture of the young woman becomes more and more prominent—by the time the twentieth picture has been shown, the image of the old woman is almost invisible. The audience can see quite clearly that each picture is different from the preceding one: They are alert and sensitive to the fact that there are changes in each drawing. What is remarkable, however, is that when they are asked what it is a drawing of, over two thirds of them (sometimes more) continue to say they have seen a picture of an old woman. The world has changed, so to speak, but their image or concept of it is the same! Despite the fact that the picture of the young woman is virtually crying out to be seen, they cling to their first interpretation of the picture.

The old woman/young woman picture takes unfair advantage (unfair if you are seeing it for the first time) of the very ability that we have as normal adults that makes us smart. We are used to identifying pictures of people quickly and accurately, and we are normally right when we look at a picture and identify it. "It's a picture of an old woman, right?" "Right on—it's an old woman." Alas, the very ability that makes us smart also makes us stupid.

When we look at an ambiguous picture and identify an image, our mind plays a trick on us—it goes to sleep. When we are satisfied that we have identified something correctly, which is normally the case, our mind not only shuts down ("Ah, yes, it's an old woman") but it also *blocks out* or excludes alternative interpretations of the picture. In a sense, the mind is lulled into a state of security or inaction because of our certainty that we have solved the problem. But what can be unsettling to us when the problem is a creative or complex one is the tendency of the mind to refuse to consider another way of looking at the problem. Once we decide that it's a picture of an old woman, that's it. We are locked into our first interpretation of the picture, and rigidly. We have been victimized by a mind-set. The maddening party game known as Chinese numbers also illustrates this point, and in an even more interesting way.

Chinese Numbers as a Test of Rigidity

The word rigidity is a pretty good synonym for stupidity, although you might not find it listed as a synonym in the average thesaurus. To be a normal adult person is to sometimes be rigid and to lack flexibility. Rigidity in the way we think is not only normal—it is a pervasive problem in effective management, particularly with regard to the development of good managerial and organizational strategies. In management seminars and classes I've used the game of Chinese numbers to illustrate how rigidity can get in the way of creative thinking and how emotional processes can make rigidity even worse.

I start the game by making an announcement something like, "Chinese numbers is a numbers game, and it's called Chinese numbers because of its inscrutable Oriental qualities that are very difficult for Occidental minds like ours to fathom. Before I start the game, I'd like to collect about a dozen pens and pencils from you." The collection of the pens and pencils proceeds with appropriate pomp and ceremony, and when it is complete I ask the participants to come to an open area in the room.

I now drop to my knees and tell the participants that I'm going to make a series of Chinese numbers on the floor. "All of the numbers are between zero and ten, including zero and ten, and all of the numbers are whole numbers—no decimals or fractions to confuse you. After I make a number, I'd like you to look at it for a while, and then if you think you know what it is—or if you'd just like to take a guess—go ahead and tell me. When you get the number right, I'll tell you."

I now make a great show of arranging the pens and pencils in groups, with some crossed, and some uncrossed. After completing the arrangement, while casually leaning on one hand, I ask if anyone can identify the number. Many *guesses* are offered, until the correct number is named, with the "winner" uncertain as to how she chose the right answer. Saying nothing, I continue to make new arrangements of the pens and pencils. Bewilderment gives way to frustration, as literally dozens of incorrect guesses are made—until the first person finally learns how to read the numbers.*

People's reactions when they learn how the numbers are made are a study in consternation: they laugh, they express hilarious disgust, and—the point here—they begin thinking about the meaning of the game. In the discussion that follows several points emerge, among them the fact that the harder we try, the harder the game gets. "You can't see the forest for the trees," one participant has observed, meaning that as we concentrate harder on the arrangements of pens and pencils, we become all the less likely to see the fingers that the leader has placed on the floor.

We sometimes have the illusion as we look out at our world that we are seeing everything that is going on around us: that we are literally taking a picture or a photograph of everything in our immediate environment, through our eyes. The reality is that we are seeing only a tiny portion of all the information (visual and otherwise) that is out there for us to process and digest. We quite literally suffer from *tunnel vision*: We see what our eyes are focused on, and not much else. Only a small proportion of all the information out there is actually being dealt with, although the subjective feeling that most of us have is that we are dealing with all of it. Perception is highly selective: We see only what we are looking for.

---

* The mislead in Chinese numbers is the collection of pens and pencils, which have nothing to do with the actual number. The "number" is displayed by the leader, who, when leaning on his hand, points a certain number of fingers on the floor. The fingers should be front and center, so that they are clearly visible to members of the audience. When you play Chinese numbers be sure to ask members of the audience not to say how the numbers are made when they first learn how to read them, or much of the suspense of the game will be spoiled.

When we play Chinese numbers, we focus on the pens and pencils, and when we fail to learn how the numbers are made, we try all the harder, since most of us have learned that the road to treasured success is to redouble our efforts when we fail. Alas, this effort also makes us stupid, since we fail to look around: We do not see the fingers that the devilish leader has placed on the floor.

In addition to the common illusion that we are seeing everything that is going on is the natural human tendency to *intensify* a perceptual strategy that is failing. Several researchers, including Henry Mintzberg[3] and Barry Shaw,[4] have studied this phenomenon and its effects on management. Executives often increase their commitment to a past strategy that is failing rather than consider changing the strategy and will even go so far as to replace key managers rather than modify the strategy. When we fail to read Chinese numbers, we go through exactly the same process that organizations do when they cling rigidly to a failed strategy.

People who fail to learn how to read Chinese numbers almost without exception get mad. They may deny it or pretend that they are cool and calm, but with very few exceptions they get angry. Some may lose their cool and begin saying things like, "This is a stupid damned game anyway. I'm paying good money to attend this seminar, and you're making me play a stupid game like Chinese numbers." So much for the denunciations of the game—the anger being expressed is what psychologists call a *masking emotion*: The anger masks or disguises a deeper and very unpleasant emotion, namely, fear.

Fear is a very difficult emotion for almost anyone to experience. It produces a range of physiological reactions: an excruciating sense of anxiety, sweating, palpitations, "butterflies" in the stomach, and overall agitation and arousal. One of the most unpleasant fears that many of us have is that we are actually stupid and incompetent, that our professional or social success is really due to luck or chance, and that we have succeeded largely because we have pulled the wool over the eyes of the so-called significant others around us.

The origins of this fear are many—discounting and negative remarks from parents, teachers, and supervisors are a major source—but whatever its origins, the fear itself is most unpleasant to deal with. When fear is triggered by our failure to learn to read Chinese numbers or by any other failure experience, the fear is quickly and automatically masked by or covered up with anger. It is often much easier to be angry with something "out there," like Chinese numbers, our spouse, or a garbage can, than it is to acknowledge the gut-grinding and relentless fear within us. When we grow angry with a "stupid game like Chinese numbers," we externalize the problem and neatly avoid having to take responsibility for our failure.

Once we get mad we become even less likely to succeed at learning how to read the numbers. The anger and underlying fear are so disruptive that many will simply walk away from the game rather than deal with the consequences of failure. Those who stay are so agitated that they are unable to think clearly: It is well documented that one of the immediate outcomes of a high level of stress is to reduce intellectual functioning to a much more primitive level.[5] Anger may have its uses in dealing with problems, but the development of clear and creative (and effective) strategies for solving problems is obviously not one of them.

The Four-Dots Puzzle

"I'd like you to draw four dots on a sheet of paper, in exactly the same way that I'm drawing them on the board now. Now, I'm going to give you a simple set of instructions that I'd like you to carry out. I'd like you to connect all four of the dots you've drawn, using no more that *three* straight lines that must not cross each other. The figure you draw to connect the dots must have no open sides in it. Please go ahead and do it."

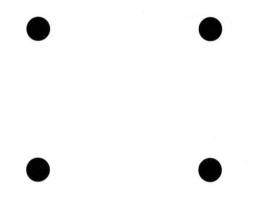

We Box Ourselves In

"I'd like you to draw four dots on a sheet of paper," I say to members of a creative-thinking seminar, "in exactly the same way that I'm drawing them on the board now." I then draw a neat pattern of dots, as illustrated above. After the participants finish drawing their dots, I say, "Now, I'm going to give you a simple set of instructions that I'd like you to carry out. I'd like you to connect all four of the dots you've drawn, using no more than *three* straight lines that must not cross each other. The figure you draw to connect the dots must have no open sides in it. Please go ahead and do it."

This instruction invites questions: "We can only use *straight* lines?" The answer is yes. "You mean we can't use more than three straight lines?" The answer, yes. I also ask participants not to show their answers to others, and they dutifully comply. As some get the answer and smiles flash around the room, I begin giving hints to those still working on the problem. "You've got to stop thinking square, or you can't do it." "You're square thinkers—that's the problem." These hints help several who have been stumped by the problem, and soon most of them have the answer, as illustrated on page 46.

In the discussion that follows, habits of mind that are normal and powerful are identified. Although my opening instructions never mentioned the words square or rectangle, without exception the members of the group immediately saw just such a shape as they were drawing their dots: They mentally filled in the gaps and fixed the image of the square in their minds securely and immediately. Truly, they boxed themselves in. Once they saw a square or rectangle, they *assumed* that they had to stay within its boundaries, and then the puzzle became difficult.

The introduction of the word assumption allows me to dust off the well-known joke about the word assume: that when we assume, it makes an "ass" out of "u" and "me." The old, slightly lame joke produces predictable groans, but it also serves to make an important point. When the participants are asked how they made their creative breakthroughs in the process of solving the problem, most acknowledge that it occurred when they stopped thinking square and began to look beyond the boundary of the dots.

The Four-Dots Puzzle Solution

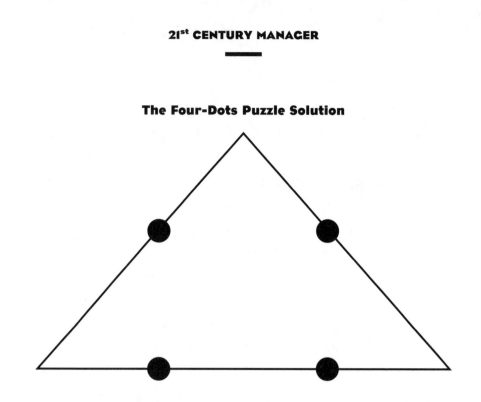

On the Relationship Between Competence and Creativity/Flexibility

Psychologists have known for many years that there is very little relationship between intelligence, as measured by standardized tests of intelligence, and creativity/flexibility. Research has shown conclusively that above a standardized intelligence score (or IQ) of 120, there is no relationship to speak of. A reasonably high level of intelligence seems to be a *precondition* for the development of creative thinking but certainly is not a guarantee that creative ability will develop or unfold.

Games like Chinese numbers demonstrate this clearly. A group of highly intelligent adults will struggle for minutes (indeed, for hours!) before they learn to read the numbers. It is very difficult to predict who will learn to read them first: Often it is people with highly specialized training and advanced degrees in mathematics or computer science who have the most difficulty, but liberal arts majors also flounder (we are ecumenical when it comes to laying the blame). Children tend to learn to read the numbers more rapidly than do adults, but if children do not succeed at the game, they rapidly do a childish thing: They quit and move on to something else.

Intellectual competence, accompanied by very specialized or technical training, sometimes produces tunnel vision, or rigidity, that can lead to strategic failure and even the bankruptcy of a business. What happened to Chrysler Corporation in the 1970s and 1980s is a case in point. Historically, Chrysler had been headed by intelligent executives with strong competencies in engineering and accounting. They stressed engineering excellence in all the vehicles Chrysler produced, and for many years the company manufactured sturdy cars and trucks that were marvels of mechanical perfection. The company's cars were as solid as tanks, cynics noted, but they also looked like tanks. Perhaps coincidentally, the company's tank division prospered while the rest of the firm began to flounder. Chrysler had neglected attractive design and styling and its marketing was weak—both critical success factors, or CSFs, in the auto industry. The company began to lose market share to both foreign and domestic competitors: by the late 1980s it was in desperate shape.

While other factors—including aging plants, a weak line of large luxury cars, and high labor costs—contributed to the decline of Chrysler, most analysts agree that its preoccupation with engineering and its relative inattention to more critical CSFs were the major causes of its problems. When the company brought in the aggressive and marketing-oriented Lee Iacocca as its chief executive officer it broke the string of engineering/accounting-oriented CEOs, and it undoubtedly saved its bacon. Iacocca moved rapidly, and some say ruthlessly, to downsize the company and focus on its most popular models. He also went on national television and made strong personal appeals for Chrysler cars, which was totally unprecedented in the history of the company.

No professional group has a monopoly on rigidity, of course, but a reasonable case can be made for the validity of the Peter Principle[6]: that in many organizations, especially vertical ones, individuals are promoted to positions of increasing seniority until they demonstrate so much incompetence that they can no longer be promoted. A major cause of a company's incompetence is quite obviously the promotion of highly specialized and somewhat rigid people who have succeeded in specialized jobs to executive positions requiring creativity and flexibility—where they fail.

The characteristics of rigidity, particularly in its extreme form, are probably better understood by social scientists than are the characteristics of creativity. In any event, the person or organization that is rigid to an unusual or exaggerated degree will usually have some or all of the following characteristics:

1. Cling to established ways of doing things. "We're doing it this way because we've always done it that way." "My great-grandfather said

this was the only way to do it, and by god that's how we're going to do it."

2. Suspicious of and highly resistant to change. "All this high-tech stuff going on—what's the world coming to?" "Things just aren't like they used to be in the good old days."

3. Dogmatic[7] and self-righteous. "My way's the only way, and my way is right." "We're not the problem; it's the other guys who screwed up."

4. Hold a view of the world as threatening and fail to see new opportunities. "Life is a jungle, and you gotta be tough just to survive." "Those little home computers are a dumb idea—they'll never catch on."

5. React badly to stress. "No problem is too small for us to panic over."

6. Function well enough in the short run, but it will usually fail in the long run. "Ah, we're doing okay making widgets. We don't have to worry about making new products."

The world of a rigid person or organization is a black-white, no-shades-of-gray world, and such an organization will inevitably spend a great deal of its time *reacting* to problems: fighting fire after fire, coping with crisis after crisis, and scrambling just to stay alive or in business.

Why Mind-Sets Persist: The Power of Self-Fulfilling Prophecy

It is a logical and fair question, when we see an otherwise bright person persist rigidly with a failed strategy, completely fail to see the fingers on the floor in Chinese numbers, see only one image in the young woman/old woman picture, or box themselves in the four-dots exercise, to ask *why* mind-sets are so powerfully persistent. A big chunk of the answer lies in the concept of *self-fulfilling prophecy*, which was popularized in the best-selling book *Pygmalion in the Classroom*, by Robert Rosenthal and Lenore Jacobsen.[8] Some three decades after the completion of their original research, their findings are as valid as ever.

In the original Pygmalion studies, teachers of elementary school children were told that certain of their students (all of whom had taken a standardized intelligence test early in the school year) showed unusual intellectual promise or potential and could be expected to show gains in intelligence test scores at the end of the year. Unbeknownst to the teachers, the students with "potential" had in fact been chosen completely at random, with no psychological or educational basis whatsoever. What is so startling about this research is that the students who had been identified as promising did indeed show significantly greater gains in intelligence (as measured by the test) at the end of the school year than did students who had not been chosen.

What miracle occurred here? Precisely the miracle of mind-set or self-fulfilling prophecy, of course. The teachers tended to pay more attention to, spend more time with, and generally expect more of the students who had been chosen. The teachers were not aware or conscious of this and often denied that they had done anything extraordinary or unusual with chosen students. Nonetheless, the findings were real and clearly demonstrate the power of self-fulfilling prophecy, in this case in the form of a positive prejudice.

In what subtle but important ways did the teachers communicate to their students that they expected good things from them? How did the students decipher that more was expected and then fulfill their teachers' expectations? Some factors are not particularly mysterious—more time, more attention, and perhaps more praise—but other factors may never be fully known. It is a good bet, however, that 70 to 80 percent of the answer lies in the large portion of communication that is nonverbal: 70 to 80 percent. *What* we say with words is only a small portion of communication; *how* we communicate with nonverbal signals—gestures, facial expressions, friendly pats and hugs, and attitude—is far and away the biggest chunk.

Since the chosen students in Rosenthal and Jacobsen's research were generally not stupid, they picked up on the positive nonverbal signals they were getting from their teachers, and they responded accordingly. Is there one of us who does not respond well when an important person in our lives thinks well of us? Positive expectations produce positive results, which is a worthwhile message for any teacher or manager, but negative expectations have nasty results, and this is an absolutely critical message for every modern manager.

For those of us who have worked for someone who thinks we are stupid (or clutzy, or lazy, or irresponsible), which is just about all of us at one time or another, we have experienced the disastrous negative impact of self-fulfilling prophecy—as did Jean Smith in the story that introduces this chapter. Negative self-fulfilling prophecies are negative prejudices, and in a world of niceness and political correctness, while they may not be stated openly, they are nonetheless real and powerful. Bill Roberts brought about what he believed to be true, that women are emotional and undependable: After Jean broke down in his office, his mind-set about women became more rigid than ever.

Did Jean Smith see, and feel, his prejudicial mind-set? Was this the final straw that broke the proverbial camel's back? Did a bright and hard-working person become another victim of a self-fulfilling prophecy? What can be done to weaken the power of mind-sets, to be less judgmental, to be more open-minded in a world of mind-sets, and to thereby become a better and more flexible manager? A sensible first step is to review some rather common managerial mind-sets rooted in the wisdom of the vertical organization with a view to understanding them and uprooting them.

The Mind-Sets of the Past

The twenty-first century beckons, and the nineteenth lingers. The long, long history of the hierarchical organization has produced a series of managerial mind-sets that over the decades have acquired all of the rigidity of cast iron but must now be cracked and discarded. Perhaps the most common among these are the following:

1. *"I am the boss."* The manager who announces to employees that he or she is the boss may wish to be treated with the reverence due a deity but in the twenty-first century is more likely to enjoy irreverence, including behind-the-back laughter. Employees these days don't waste time getting mad at the boss; in the words of the cliché, they just get even. Bosses who try to boss must get bossier and bossier. And cynics note that boss is a four-letter word.

The first mind-set of the nineteenth century to go the way of the Dodo bird in the twenty-first is the word boss. Bosses are now facilitators, coaches, and team cheerleaders, and employees are associates, colleagues, and valued co-workers. This changing terminology is not just a matter of political correctness—it reflects a historical change in the use of power and authority as we will see in the remaining chapters of this book.

2. *"My employees can't handle much responsibility."* This mind-set reflects a management style that embodies an unwillingness to delegate appropriately and effectively. Since employees are not stupid, when they see clearly that a manager will not entrust them with responsibility, they become angry and are likely to behave irresponsibly. "Treat a man like a dog, and he'll act like a dog," the famous football coach Vince Lombardi once said.

This is not to suggest for a moment that inexperienced, untrained employees should immediately be given the keys to the kingdom: Chaos might immediately result, again fulfilling a prophecy. When delegation follows appropriate counseling, coaching, and training, however, it not only empowers the workforce but it can also transform the entire organization.

3. *"I am an expert in this area."* The hierarchical, functional organization demands functional expertise: The accountants in the accounting department must be competent accountants; the engineers in the engineering department must be . . . well, you get the picture. In the earlier discussion of the woes of the Chrysler Corporation, excessive functionalization or specialization was a clear cause of the company's problems. Chrysler's situation was by no means unusual, since other vertical organizations found themselves in exactly the same bind—consider IBM, for instance.

The United States has had a long love affair with experts in almost every area of life: medicine, the law, relationships and marriage, child-rearing, fitness, and microbiology. The love affair is ending, however, as all affairs do, and nowhere more dramatically than in industry. In the twenty-first century, intelligent, flexible *generalists* will be the hottest commodity on the job market—a fact that some executives and hiring specialists (yes, more experts!) have already begun to realize. The time has come for more global vision and less tunnel vision, more good management and less micromanagement.

Piet Hen (the poet, not the famous chicken) summed it up nicely in these well-known words:

> "Experts have their expert fun
> Ex cathedra telling one
> Just why nothing can be done."[9]

4. *"I will talk, and you will listen."* This mind-set translates directly into a management style that is not only obsolete but disastrous.

Anyone who is not listened to, or whose inputs are not valued, will feel discounted. Discounted people can be counted upon to behave in disruptive and childish ways, and another self-fulfilling prophecy has been confirmed. Talking and not listening is based upon the need to hold on to power.

Let's stop a moment. These four mind-sets all have a common basis, and that is *fear*: the fear of losing control, of giving up power. Managers and executives have long displayed high N.P., or need for power, a motivational concept developed by David McClelland at Harvard University, while they tend to be rather low in N'Aff, or the need for affiliation (love, relationships, and friendship). Giving up formal power is paramount for empowering workers and teams in an organization. Neurotic attempts to hold on to formal authority in the corporations of the twenty-first century are sure to be self-defeating, and the manager who attempts to cling to power will surely lose it.

The founding fathers of the United States realized all too clearly what an intoxicating, addictive, and abusive thing power can be, and they developed an entire constitution to control its use. What we have recognized for over two centuries as a constitutional democracy we are beginning to recognize in our major corporations: Truly, all power must be shared for the good of most of the people, most of the time, if I may coin an expression.* Now on to the final two mind-sets.

---

* British historian Lord Acton coined the most pithy and best-known expression about the lure of power: "Power tends to corrupt, and absolute power corrupts absolutely."[10]

5. *"Socializing with employees is a waste of time."* The coffee breaks, the company party, and the work-based slow-pitch softball team are virtually American institutions, yet the notion persists in some management circles that at-work fraternization and socialization are wasteful and counterproductive. Fifty years of research by social scientists and the Hawthorne studies be damned, "We've got to put a stop to this talking on the job."

Like many mind-sets, the talking-is-a-waste-of-time notion *does* contain a kernel of truth: Idle chatter and gossip, too many personal phone calls, and frequent interruptions of work by personal business *can* be disruptive and unproductive and need to be dealt with proactively and effectively by concerned management. Despite this disclaimer, the promotion of effective socialization is a set of management skills that will become increasingly necessary in the new organizational age.

6. *"All these women, old folks, temps, and minority group members in the workforce are a real problem."* The twentieth century will undoubtedly be recorded by historians as the last great hurrah of the white male manager, both for good and for bad. Near the close of the century, the glass ceiling for women and members of minority groups is still a fact (in 1995 well over 95 percent of all corporate CEOs were white males), but the cracks are beginning to show. The greatest problem that women and members of minority groups in an increasingly diverse workforce still face is the one exemplified in the case that opens this chapter: the mind-set known as prejudice, or stereotyping.

Since the diversity of the workplace will in fact increase, the challenge for twenty-first-century management will be to cope with it constructively and flexibly, make it a strength, and deal with it as a dynamic and continuing fact of American life.

The Mind-Sets of the Future: Openness and Flexibility as a Managerial Value

Mind-sets are not mindless or accidental; instead they reflect the values and the needs of organizations and societies. Organizations that are tall, rigid, vertical hierarchies need specialists, bosses, and executives who make decisions and employees who accept them. Authoritarian societies needed a ruling class. The mind-sets of the past were functional and adaptive in the world of the past, a world of relative stability and not much change.

The world of the future promises more change, more diversity, and the continuing emergence of a global business community. What this new world values and needs is an attitude of openness to change and the managerial skills of flexibility and proactive problem solving that are necessary to cope with change. Henry David Thoreau once said, "It is never too late to give up our prejudices,"[11] and in the emerging world of the twenty-first century, that statement has never been more true.

TWENTY-FIRST-CENTURY MANAGEMENT IN ACTION

Some Mind-Openers for Regular Use

There seems to be little agreement among the gurus of the age (psychologists, psychiatrists, newspaper advice columnists, clerics, and every management consultant who has ever written a book) about exactly what we mortals can do to overcome our mind-sets and prejudices. As I have noted repeatedly, normal people have a normal share of habits-of-mind, and most of us will have blind spots and automatic tendencies until the day we die. Despite the abundance of material that has been written (or recorded) on the subject of becoming more flexible, creative, and open-minded, the following modest list of suggestions is offered as a sensible list of things that most of us *can do* (the All-American attitude, if ever there was one) to live in a more open and flexible way:

Don't compare yourself to anyone else. If there is a habit of mind that is more common and more self-defeating than that of comparing oneself to others that any reader knows of, please send in cards and letters at once. We are ourselves and no one else. We need to find what abilities, gifts, and interests we have and develop those. Despite the presence of some six billion others on this planet, each of us is unique.

Lest these statements be discounted as simple-minded platitudes, since they are hardly unique to this book, consider for a moment the case of an individual who is convinced that he or she is a "world champion" in some category—sex appeal, intelligence, or athleticism. For everyone determined to be a champion, there are six billion challengers, so world champions typically don't stay on top for long. The world-champion mind-set can lead to a life of workaholism, compulsive overachievement, and chronic exhaustion. Life is not a situation that we get out of alive anyway, say the cynics.

Find something to like, do it well, and enjoy doing it. Enjoy the freedom and flexibility of not having to compete with the rest of the human race. Learn to enjoy life a little.

Keep fit and stay fit. Good physical health is the key to just about everything else. Eat sensibly, exercise regularly, and keep body weight down. Lean-and-mean twenty-first-century organizations need lean people. Much of the world faces the challenge of finding enough food to eat, but Americans face the challenge of eating less. While an abundance of research shows that physically healthy people also tend to be mentally fit (alert, relaxed, open to new ideas, and in good touch with reality), as Americans we have been subjected to such a torrent of information on this topic that this particular slice of advice has been kept very slim, indeed.

Get in touch with reality, especially Mother Nature. Even in the most urbanized jungle, natural beauty awaits us every day: trees, and birds, and snowflakes, and stars. The first warm spring days fill the streets of every city in America with people enjoying the beauty of Mother Nature, and SAD (seasonal affective disorder) disappears for another year. Contact with growing and living things (sometimes including children, and almost always pets) in our working and home environments is relaxing and healthy and opens us to new stimuli and new ideas, many of them emerging from the creative realm of the unconscious. Many a creative breakthrough has been made while the learned manager was walking along a leafy trail in the woods, thinking about nothing in particular and enjoying the world we live in. I will *not* offend the intelligence of my readers by reminding them to smell the roses along the way.

Give up a hated job, if at all possible. The boring, abusive, distasteful, and hated job takes up eight hours a day in direct discomfort and the remaining sixteen in agonizing, escape activities, sleeplessness, and ongoing therapy. The hated job destroys creativity and flexibility and focuses our minds in dreadfully unhealthy ways. Obsession, paranoia, chronic anxiety, homicidal rage, and other diagnosable reactions can occur after prolonged exposure to a hated work environment.

If it is not possible to give up a hated job for practical reasons, at the very least a résumé can be updated and a job search begun. These activities can often serve as a healthy antidote to the toxic effects of an unhealthy work environment. I truly wish I had such good advice to give the chronically unemployed: This will have to be the subject of another book.

Discover the liberating power of humor. "Laughter is the best medicine," the saying goes. And so it is. Humor heals, releases tension, and opens the windows of the mind. The most gentle and liberating humor is that directed at ourselves: our foibles, failures, and fallibility. All humor is not necessarily healing and helpful, however. Jokes that "put down" or discount other individuals or groups often increase tension and harden prejudice. Sexist and racist "humor" falls into this category. For the genuinely and deeply humorless person there are literally hundreds of good books of jokes available in bookstores everywhere.

Take a risk every now and again. Entrepreneurship has been described as the willingness to take risks, and entrepreneurship is the very lifeblood of the emerging global economy. Any person not willing to take risks of any kind is probably doomed to failure or at least to a pretty dull and inflexible life. Fear of risk is usually accompanied by the fear of failure and the fear of making mistakes. I leave to the fertile imagination and creativity of the reader the form of the risk: an investment, a relationship, a change of employment. The choices are many.

Do problems, puzzles, and creative-thinking exercises. Graduates of my seminars and courses sometimes tell me that they don't remember a single thing I said, but they can't forget Chinese numbers. Puzzles and novel problems are great nutcrackers for really tough mind-sets. While hundreds of books are available, a particularly readable and delightful volume is *Thinkertoys*, by Michael Michalko (Berkeley, Calif.: Ten Speed Press, 1991). The book is subtitled *A Handbook of Business Creativity for the '90s* and warns prospective readers that "This book is for monkeys." What flexible and creative person could resist such a come-on?

ENDNOTES

1. Robert Burns, "To a Louse," quoted in John Bartlett, *Familiar Quotations*, 16th Ed. (Boston: Little, Brown, 1992), p. 361.

2. Robert Leeper, "The Role of Motivation in Learning: A Study of the Phenomenon of Differential Motivation Control of the Utilization of Habits," *Journal of Genetic Psychology* 46 (1935): 3-40.

3. Henry Mintzberg, "Research on Strategy Making" (paper presented at the Annual Meeting of the Academy of Management, 1972).

4. Barry Shaw, "Knee Deep in the Big Muddy: A Study of Escalating Commitment to a Chosen Course of Action," *Organizational Behavior and Human Performance* (June 1976).

5. See Harold Schroder, Michael Driver, and Siefried Streufert, *Human Information Processing* (New York: Holt, Rinehart and Winston, 1967).

6. Laurence Peter and Raymond Hill, *The Peter Principle* (New York: Morrow, 1969).

7. Milton Rokeach, *The Open and Closed Mind* (New York: Basic Books, 1960).

8. Robert Rosenthal and Lenore Jacobsen, *Pygmalion in the Classroom.* (New York: Holt, Rinehart and Winston, 1968).

9. This author's work is not found in the usual scholarly references: check out your local bathroom walls.

10. Lord Acton, "Letter to Bishop Mandell Creighton," quoted in Bartlett, p. 521.

11. Henry David Thoreau, "Walden, 1, Economy," quoted in Bartlett, p. 478.

3

POSITIVE AND PROACTIVE PROBLEM-SOLVING SKILLS (PPPS) FOR EVERY MANAGER

Gus the Creative Rehabber

Dr. Jim Williams left the academic world in 1994 to pursue a full-time hobby: rehabbing (gutting and restoring) the beautiful old brick homes that abound in his inner-city neighborhood in Baltimore, Maryland. He had discovered that he loves to take a nineteenth-century structure and transform it into a beautiful new home—with the same brick shell and facade—suitable for civilized occupancy in the twenty-first century.

The foreman of his crew of ten men and women is a slight, energetic 55-year-old man, Gus Partain, whose mysterious and multitalented background was equaled only by the marvelous quality and solid sensibility of his work. Gus is indeed a versatile craftsman—painter and plumber, electrician and drywall hanger, carpenter and tuckpointer—he can do it all, surpassing the most stringent building inspector's examination with ease. He is also a graduate of the American Penal System.

In an earlier life (or "in my misspent youth," as Gus liked to say), he had been a master craftsman of another kind: He was the finest arsonist in the state of Maryland ("Burned 'em for a thousand bucks a pop, and no one but me—and the owner—know they'd been torched," he told Jim), and a gifted jewelry store thief who was caught only after he had robbed seven different stores in Maryland and Virginia. "Would never have done time if I hadn't shot off my big mouth about my last job in Roanoke," he said, "and one of my buddies turned me in for the reward." His jewelry store robberies were marked by meticulous planning: binocular surveillance of the premises, careful noting of delivery and departure times, and a strategic choice of the best possible break-in time. Gus could pick any known combination of locks, open the most foolproof safes, and disarm the most sophisticated burglar-alarm systems. He was clearly a genius, although somewhat misguided.

Gus brought these same gifts to rehabbing and to the management of Jim's crew, in his maturity. His watchword, known to all members of the crew, is "think fast, and move slowly." And think he does: Every rehab project, from the smallest painting job to the restoration of an entire building, is marked by careful planning, superb coordination of the rehab team ("What a team," he says with real pride), and careful execution of the work, from stripping old plaster off brick walls to touch-up painting. Each member of the team is trained in at least two or three skills: The best are highly competent in several after a year on the crew. Each job is completed on schedule, or very close to the final time projection, even though one of the iron laws of rehabbing old buildings is that every job takes approximately three times as long as the most liberal time estimate. The cost is also an eye opener: about $25 a square foot from start to finish, compared to over $40 for most other contractors. Dr. Jim Williams is getting a mighty big bang for his buck and most of the credit is due to the versatility and management skills of Gus Partain.[1]

What is so easily understandable and touchingly human as the impulse to lock the barn door after the horse has escaped? The old adage lives on, decade after decade, because it so accurately describes much human behavior: the failure to anticipate a problem, the failure to deal with it effectively, and the failure to develop management skills to prevent it from happening again. Millions and millions of Americans wait until April 15 to file their tax returns, and the U.S. Postal Service obliges them by arranging for last-minute pickups of returns at hundreds of locations throughout the nation. Millions more avail themselves of the automatic six-month extension and still file frantically at the last minute. Millions more do not file at all and get into all sorts of trouble with the omnipotent agents of the IRS, when almost any sort of coherent return would have prevented the problem.

April 15 is perhaps the best publicized, and worst kept, deadline in American society. We all know about it, but the procrastinating behavior of the average taxpayer* illustrates all too clearly that many of us *react* or *overreact* to problem situations that are often predictable and fail to

---

* I have one or two incredibly proactive friends who file their returns (by computer) by February 15 each year—their bodies (and their computers!) should be preserved for posterity.

cope effectively with situations that can (and must) be coped with. In the emerging world of free, flat, fair, and flexible organizations, reactive and overreactive behavior can become disastrous when unpredictable and rapidly changing problems must be dealt with. Proactive and effective problem-solving behavior, on the other hand, is all but indispensable in the complex and globalized organizational world that will be a part of the twenty-first century.

A Continuum of
Managerial Problem Solving

The procrastinating behavior of millions of Americans regarding the annual tax-return deadline (which follows April Fools' Day by only two weeks) is a common example of *reactive* behavior or management, which is the first response many of us make to emerging or ongoing problems. Procrastination is so common in so many environments, including organizational environments, that it surely must top any list of self-defeating avoidance behaviors. Avoidance is a general term, largely self-explanatory, that describes the principal behaviors that are found in a reactive pattern: procrastination, lying, denial, rationalization, and wishful thinking. Avoidance in all its forms is motivated by *fear*: fear of conflict, fear of failure, fear of risk, and fear of fear; and it has a universal and totally predictable outcome, which is that it makes all types of problems worse and often leads to *overreactive* or crisis management (see the continuum of managerial problem-solving styles on page 67).

Wishful thinking is a particularly self-defeating mind-set that has been with us since Adam and Eve, as opposed to those described in

A Continuum of Managerial Problem-Solving Styles

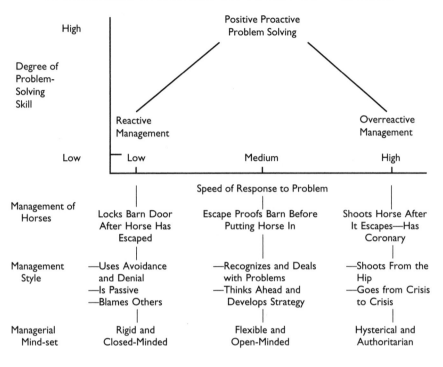

Chapter Two—as most wishful thinkers realize at bottom. The hopeful thought that a problem will just go away makes it all too easy to rationalize total inaction: a failure to respond in any constructive way to the development or arrival of a problem. Like any other mind-set, wishful thinking has a kernel of truth in it, since some problems *do* go away or at least diminish over time. Untreated wounds sometimes heal themselves over time but more often kill or maim the wounded. Floods eventually go away, but the unprotected inhabitants of a flood plain are often swept away first. Employees with personal problems often overcome them even when management fails to intervene, but the process of getting work done usually suffers in both the short and long run.

The eternal attraction of all forms of avoidance, including wishful thinking, is that it will buy us a little time. Take, for instance, Joe, who has been coming to work late (and later, and later) because of some "temporary personal problems," and his hopeful manager, Robert, who thinks that if he just waits it out for a little while and maintains pleasant relations with Joe in the meantime, the problem will soon be over. Joe will start coming in on time again, and his work will get done; the customer who has called the company twice about a delayed shipment of agricultural chemicals can be held off for another day or two (we'll wait for a while to return her calls), and in the meantime the shipment will surely arrive and the problem will be solved.

Ah, the attraction, and the folly of reactive management on the low end of the continuum, because . . . Joe sees all too clearly that behind the facade of pleasantness and niceness that Robert's presenting to him daily, there beats the heart of a truly gutless wonder. He takes advantage of management that he knows will be totally—and slowly—reactive and do absolutely nothing about his "temporary" problem. Soon Joe is coming in three days a week while being paid for five, and the employee is successfully managing the manager who eventually develops a murderous rage toward the bright but troubled person who is taking advantage of him. The customer who needs her agricultural chemicals may indeed get her shipment while Robert stalls, but she knows all too well why her calls are not being returned and her respect for the company is forever diminished. In fact, she probably will turn to a company—a competitor—that returns her calls when orders are delayed.

The fear that lies behind a reactive pattern of avoidance is usually a *neurotic* fear; that is to say, it is not based on reality. If Robert confronted Joe proactively, the odds are very good that Joe would shape up and begin coming in on time and respect management more at the same time. The fear of confrontation and the accompanying risk of being disliked is very common among adults (second only, in most surveys, to the fear of public speaking) and is a major reason why managers avoid confronting problems of the two-legged variety.

One of the fascinating characteristics of a neurotic fear, which is usually rooted in the helplessness and vulnerability of childhood, is that a person in the grip of such a fear will bring about the very thing that he or she fears. Neurotic fears, such as the fear of being disliked and the fear of confrontation, not only lead to avoidance of problems and constructive actions but also result in paralysis: The fear does not go away but actually grows stronger over time. The longer Robert procrastinates, the more the problem begins to magnify in his mind—the proverbial molehill becoming a mountain—and the less likely he is to take action.[2]

Reactive management is also aided and abetted by the amazing human ability for self-deception, the immense capacity that many of us have to justify or rationalize our inaction (or inappropriate actions). Robert undoubtedly used some familiar mind-sets to explain his behavior: "The problem's temporary; it'll soon get better." Right. "I'll deal with him tomorrow, for tomorrow's another day." Shades of Scarlett O'Hara! "It's all the fault of the human resource department—they should've done something by now." There we go: self-righteously blame the other guy and deny all responsibility for the problem.

Joe, for his part, undoubtedly played his own mind games. "I deserve a little time off because I've worked so hard for this unfeeling organization." Two days a week ought to be about right, eh? "Robert is so gutless he deserves to be taken advantage of." The mind-set of a child in an adult body, again not an uncommon phenomenon in our society. "Everybody else is getting away with it around here, so I guess I will too."

Because Joe has not been confronted about coming in late, for example, and Robert literally turns his back when Joe finally does arrive for work, Joe receives the clear message that his behavior is not going to be questioned. He may know better, at bottom, but reactive and gutless management that avoids dealing with the problem behavior will progressively lull Joe into a sense of security.

When the confrontation finally does take place, it will be a doozy and have all the characteristics of *overreactive* management—way over on the other side of the continuum—with its accompanying negativity and emotionality. Robert loses his cool and begins shouting, "You worthless, malingering no-good lout—you've been getting away with murder for two years now, but by God it's going to stop!" Joe, who *has* been getting away with murder, to the total disgust of other employees—who have been waiting and hoping that Robert will eventually do something effective about this chronic problem—is shocked and startled when his wilting wimp of a manager finally works up the courage to tell him that he's going to have to begin coming in on time.

Anger begets anger, and violence often leads to violence. The hopeless twentieth-century manager who has waited much too long to deal with a problem-employee situation may at bottom hate himself for his inaction, but what he will experience in the interview with the employee is intense, *blaming* anger, which has built up to explosive levels.

Such a confrontation will not lead to effective problem solving and may even lead to what contemporary managers often fear most, namely, an armed and homicidal newly fired employee who returns to get even with management that he self-righteously believes has treated him* unfairly. It is wonderfully ironic that getting away with murder, metaphorically speaking, can sometimes lead to murder, literally speaking.

The Flip-Flop from Reactive to Overreactive Management

As you have seen, the paralysis produced by the inaction of reactive management and the lumbering and inefficient decisional processes of bureaucratized vertical hierarchies can produce a dramatic, abrupt flip-flop to *overreactive* management, where decisions are made and actions taken with almost compulsive haste. It truly becomes MBCCP (Management by Crisis, Chaos, and Panic). Overreactive management is

---

* Without exception in recent years the former employees who have returned to murder their managers have been men.

crisis management of the worst sort, because the crisis it is dealing with is a crisis that bad management has created.

While hundreds of examples of the flip-flop to overreactive management could be chosen from contemporary American industry, IBM's complete failure to anticipate the rapid decline of its core business—the mainframe computer market—in the late 1980s, and the frantic period of MBCCP that it engaged in the early 1990s while it downsized and reinvented itself, is perhaps the best example. It is fascinating that Big Blue, the quintessential blue-chip American corporation, possessor of a proud and ethical tradition and history, owner of some of the best strategic and operational minds in the world, could be so fixated on its traditional business that it quite literally missed the boat when high-powered PCs took over the computer market. Part of the problem was its mind-set ("IBM makes mainframe computers and an occasional PC) as discussed earlier, but analysts now agree that a bigger part was its inflexible corporate structure. Big Blue became just plain blue, and almost bankrupt too, and all in the space of a couple of years.[3]

Pride goeth before a fall, and MBCCP cometh, even for the biggest company. IBM had plenty of company in its corporate comeuppance, including two of the big three in the auto industry, and several giants in the airline industry (notably PanAm and Eastern) who went completely under because they did not anticipate, and failed to adapt to, major changes in their industry.

Overreactive management also stems from the short-term orientation and the quick-fix syndrome that pervades American society. While other nations, notably Japan and Germany, are much more patient with new products and ideas that do not make money immediately, woe is due the American executive who backs money-losing projects. The pressure to make money not only yearly, but quarterly, particularly in publicly held corporations that have obligations to a fickle and cynical stock market, puts terrible pressure on American executives to make a buck, and now. CEOs who lose money for their companies do not hang around long.

The decision-making pattern that emerges from all this, particularly in the area of strategic management, puts a premium on quick decision making, the ability to *appear* decisive, and a "shoot from the hip" management style that often includes authoritarian, "tough guy" management methods. When you know your job is going to be on the line if you lose money or lose too many games in professional team sports, you will feel intense pressure to do what you have to do to win. Small wonder that our executives suffer from high levels of stress. Small wonder that they feel the need to negotiate an extravagant compensation package* before they agree to take a job they know will put them in a pressure cooker.

Just as fear reared its ugly head at the low end of the reactive continuum, it plays a major role in overreactive management, as does anxiety. Fear does many things to us, few of which are for our own good, with the exception of immediate life-threatening fear that results from the

---

* While it is well-known that American executives are highly compensated relative to their international counterparts, I have never seen an article or book that analyzes this phenomenon in terms of perceived anticipatory stress coupled with consummate negotiating skill. In plain language, American executives know exactly what they're getting into and are very good at naming their price.

sudden presence of a fast-moving bus, for example, or an armed and dangerous-looking stranger. Real fear leads to the fight-or-flight response. Chronic anxiety is the price Americans, and Japanese, and Germans, and middle-class people just about everywhere in the world pay for staying in the rat race—for being achievement oriented in societies that reward achievement and scorn failure. (A consequence of this is the high rate of suicide among professionals who feel they have failed and disgraced themselves and their families.)

Neurotic fear leads to compulsive, hasty overreactions to problems of every sort and stressful management problems in particular. The chronically anxious person will be a poor decision maker because he or she will feel a powerful and immediate need to make a decision—or just do something—to reduce stress. A common example of an overreactive decision resulting from anxiety is the manager who punishes *all* employees for one employee's misbehavior. One employee steals office supplies, so an elaborate electronic surveillance system is installed that all employees must endure. Anxiety has the power to magnify any and all problems and to lure us into overreactions that often look foolish in retrospect.

The prevalence of *guilt* among adults in our society is yet another reason for the overreaction syndrome. Neurotic guilt, or the erroneous feeling that we have done something bad, often leads to avoidance behavior but can also produce hasty responses to reduce the guilt reaction, which can be most unpleasant indeed to someone experiencing it. At no time is this more true than when a manager is forced to fire someone: Employees hanging on the brink of dismissal dependably produce amazingly creative guilt trips—"You're signing my death warrant, damn you"; "Just give me one more chance, and I promise I'll do better"; "I've lost everything else, and now I'm losing my job too!" A manager who yields to guilt feelings in such a situation is, in fact, going to be doing something very bad; namely, allow himself to be manipulated into a foolish managerial decision.

It may be a bit flip, but in all fairness, the credo of the overreactive manager can be summed up in the words of a well-known little ditty:

> When in danger
>
> Or in doubt
>
> Run in circles
>
> Scream and shout.

A Positive, Proactive Problem-Solving Alternative

The alternative to reactive avoidance, and to overreactive panic, is the positive and proactive problem-solving method of management that will be the hallmark of the twenty-first-century manager. A proactive manager:

- looks ahead
- stays in charge of problems and problem solving
- does not lose his or her cool in difficult and stressful situations
- has a mind-set that unsolved problems do not go away

The gifted and sensible Gus Partain, whom you met in the story that introduces this chapter, exemplifies most of the skills that the proactive manager brings to bear in managerial decision making: He has multiple competencies and enjoys the exercise of his skills; he thinks before he acts and takes the time to develop a plan of action before beginning work; he anticipates many of the problems that inevitably develop in a complex work environment; and he empowers each and every man and woman working with him until they too possess multiple competencies and become a smoothly functioning work team.

It can be argued, and fairly, that these management skills have been around for generations, but it can also be argued with equal fairness that we are just now beginning to recognize that the *systematic* use of proactive problem-solving skills is absolutely necessary in the twenty-first-century world of fair, flat, flexible, and free organizations. The need to develop proactive skills and the mind-sets that accompany them is a logical necessity. There is nothing magical and mysterious about them, they can be learned (with practice, and over time), and they are part of a larger twenty-first-century *philosophy* of management that holds the following beliefs to be valuable and true:

1. Change will not only continue but will continue to increase in kind and quality.
2. Many problems can be anticipated, and most can be solved, with a little ingenuity and a lot of patience.
3. The ingenuity of working men and women must be stimulated and encouraged by creative and open-minded management.

4. Quick fixes, magic bullets, and "feel good" solutions are usually not effective in the long run.

5. The workforce of the future will be loyal primarily to itself, but its self-interest can be made to work for the organization.

6. Management will continue to be a demanding and stressful profession but with great personal and professional rewards.

7. Unethical treatment of people and unethical solutions to problems are destructive in the long run.

8. The future, even though it may be frightening at times, is full of opportunities.

9. The proper role of management is always to facilitate, sometimes to lead, and almost never to coerce.

10. Management problems, even though they may often be perplexing and stressful, can be a major vehicle for personal and organizational growth.

This philosophy fully recognizes that the financial health of a company is a continuing reality and that profitability must be achieved or the company will eventually go under. No serious management analyst could argue sensibly against the need for the company to make money, so the real debate centers on the best way to get there. One of the important lessons of the twentieth century has been, I hope, that short-run success is absolutely no guarantee of long-run success. Indeed, there *are* no guarantees of long-run success in business and there probably never will be.

In a well-known analogy, Michael Naylor of General Motors compares being in business and competing in free markets to being in a race—a race that never ends! If you win the race today, he says, you have only earned the right to race again tomorrow.[4] Reactive managers find this prospect hopelessly daunting, overreactive managers see it as another crisis to be dealt with, but positive and proactive managers and their organizations see this as a simple reality—and another opportunity to grow and thrive.

When Gus Partain wandered into the world of Dr. Jim Williams, he gave his Ph.D. employer an informal education in the art of proactive and positive management. While most of Gus's education had taken place in the proverbial school of hard knocks, he understands fully that when tackling a hard and complex problem, like rehabilitating an old building, *anticipation and planning* is not only a good way to begin; indeed, it is necessary. See the four steps in the positive and proactive problem-solving process on page 79.

Proactive planning, especially when it includes developing a strategy, is the first and most powerful step. Almost every management consultant who has ever given everyone else good advice asserts that good planning and strategic orientation are important in good management. There will be no disagreement with this bit of wisdom in these pages—only a modest qualifier: good planning sounds like drudgery and ends up being hard work. Entrepreneurs, as a group, love risk-taking, are achievement oriented, and are energized in a wonderful way by the process of starting new business ventures but typically hate the process of sitting down and writing a strategic business plan. Yet the research evidence is quite clear that entrepre-

The Positive and Proactive Problem-Solving Process (PPPP)

Step 1 Anticipate and Strategize
　　　　—Keep a proactive mind-set
　　　　—Learn to plan and strategize

Step 2 Develop a Proactive Action Plan to Solve the Problem
　　　　—Communicate fully with co-workers
　　　　—Be tough on the problem, not on people
　　　　—Use a coaching and counseling style
　　　　—Stay open to alternative solutions
　　　　—Take personal responsibility for the decision

Step 3 Implement the Plan
　　　　—Use participative, empowered decision making
　　　　—Make team decisions in the new age
　　　　—Recognize and deal with resistance

Step 4 Use Good Managerial Follow-Through
　　　　—Evaluate progress, and recognize failure
　　　　—Always have a contingency plan
　　　　—Avoid intensification of a failed strategy

neurs who take the time to sit down and develop a coherent, well-thought-out business plan do better than entrepreneurs who do not. Their businesses last longer and they make more money.[5] One of the reasons that a new wave of women entrepreneurs is doing well around the globe is that they are somewhat more willing and likely than are men to invest some time in planning for the business as well as less likely to take foolish risks. Planning pays because planning involves anticipation of problems, and new ventures will have problems: will they ever have problems!

The proactive mind-set that accompanies anticipation and planning is that problems are inevitable. One of the questions that is often asked new entrepreneurs by wizened gurus like me, who have failed at their own first business ventures, is whether or not there is a *fatal flaw* in the entrepreneur's proposal or plan: something that cannot normally be overcome and will kill the new enterprise, and kill it dead. Asking an entrepreneurially oriented individual to engage in such a thought process may at first seem like a bit of a "downer," but what it is in reality is a tremendously useful and powerful exercise in thinking ahead and anticipating problems.

On one occasion Gus Partain saved Jim Williams from a major financial disaster by carefully walking through a vacant brick building he had considered buying and very calmly identifying a series of structural problems, including a badly bowed outer wall that would have added up to a quarter-of-a-million dollars to the rehab effort. His grateful employer was careful to say "Thank you."

Proactive twenty-first-century management may perhaps be most simply described as management that thinks ahead. Gus Partain's remark that one should think fast and move slowly is a down-to-earth expression of a strategic and proactive mind-set. The process of thinking ahead must be followed by an appropriate action plan, however, to deal with problems faced by the organization, and this is *step two* in the positive and proactive problem-solving process. (Appropriate action as a management process is distinctly different from the hasty, often frantic, decision making that takes place in the crisis atmosphere of overreactive organizations.)

Proactive action planning has several components:

- full communication of the problem to and with co-workers
- learning to be tough on problems and stay focused on problem solving

- using a coaching and counseling management style
- consciously developing alternative solutions to problems and not getting hung up on one approach to solving a problem
- learning to take full and personal responsibility for a problem and any and all solutions, whether good or bad.

None of these can be accomplished, however, without several key management skills: an open-minded, information-seeking mind-set, as opposed to a rigid, functional, narrow, and dogmatic orientation; excellent communication ability, with heavy emphasis on the ability to communicate by *listening*; and using interactive, interpersonal problem-solving skills rather than formal authority invested in management.

Developing a good action plan is one thing—making sure it is *implemented* in the organization is often another, however. This is *step three* in the process.

Some historical lessons are more useful than others, but the battles that accompanied the introduction of computers into organizations in the 1960s and 1970s, not only in America but around the world, are a classic. One such story tells of the many executives and managers of large firms, deciding that the computer age was here to stay, developing plans to computerize routine operations and data processing. Planning was followed by purchasing: state-of-the-art computers were ordered (great, lumbering beasts by today's standards) and delivered to corporate headquarters, all neatly crated and stored, while they awaited installation.

Mysteriously and magically, the computers that had been ordered to make the company more productive and efficient grew little feet and walked out of tenth-floor windows late at night and were smashed to smithereens on the sidewalk below. The culprits were fearful and highly creative employees of the giant corporations, afraid that their jobs would disappear with the appearance of computers. Nineteenth-century management had done itself in again. The brilliant executive plan to implement computer technology not only had no employee input, but employees had been deliberately kept in the dark about the arrival of the computers. Fittingly, perhaps, it was in the still, chill of the night that the new machines performed their aeronautical wonders and flew out windows.

Remember the words of Scottish poet Robbie Burns—they have worn well over the years:

> The best laid schemes o' mice and men
> Gang aft a-gley.[6]

What went a-gley were the brilliant plans of management to install computers. The best surprise is no surprise, sayeth the Guru, and so also sayeth millions of employees who feel that there has been a basic violation of trust when revolutionary new technology is purchased without their knowledge.

Implementation is such a critical issue in every organization that it has its own particular set of management skills that *facilitate* implementation of strategic decisions and important changes. Widespread *participation* of employees in decision making, and in the management process generally, was an idea originally studied and popularized by Rensis Likert of the Institute for Social Research at the University of Michigan. His studies showed that when participative management is implemented in an organization, morale among employees goes up immediately and productivity eventually follows, if participation is given time to work. Productivity gains lag behind morale—typically by about a year—because workers need time to overcome fear and suspicion and to adapt to more challenging and interesting jobs.[7]

The success of participative management techniques, which has been documented in dozens of subsequent studies, is an important conceptual foundation of team management and employee empowerment. Employees who feel empowered, because they have *real* responsibility and a *real* voice in the decision-making process of their company, not only help make decisions—they help implement them. The result of increased information and more inputs in the decision-making process are reduced *resistance* to an important decision and more realistic and practical decisions.

The *fourth* and final step in the proactive and positive problem-solving process is another basic management task, lacking in glamour perhaps but chock full of necessity: using good managerial follow-through. Follow-through means a number of things, but first it means *evaluating progress*. Has the new computer speeded data processing and increased efficiency? If not, why not? Did the tardy employee who promised his manager that he would begin coming on time keep his promise? If not, why not? If things are on schedule and employees are coming in on time, follow-through means continuing to keep an eye on things.

The mind-set supporting good follow-through is consistent with that which supports positive and proactive problem-solving: that problems will be with us constantly and that every problem represents an opportunity for improvement. A Japanese epigram describes it perfectly: "Every defect is a treasure."[8] Treasure or not, when a defect is revealed by good follow-through, action needs to be taken. Despite the fatal flaws that may occasionally lead to the total failure of a business, most defects can be solved by vigilant evaluation and good follow-through.

Failure to Follow Through

Isn't changing a strategy that is failing something that any intelligent person or organization would do as soon as it became obvious that the strategy was failing? The reality, however, is all too often exactly what happens in Chinese numbers when a player fails to see how the numbers are in fact made. There is escalation of commitment to or intensification of a failed strategy. Follow-through is abandoned. This all-too-normal mind-set is a major reason why both managers and organizations stumble along reactively with a bad strategy when good sense dictates abandoning it, making major modifications, or replacing it with a new strategy.

Even nations as rich and powerful as the United States can easily fall victim to the folly of escalation of commitment. (The experience of this nation in Vietnam, over a twenty-year period, is a classic example. We continued to pour money and military personnel into the war in Vietnam, even though it became increasingly obvious that a military solution was

stress of crisis management. Proactive and positive managerial problem solving is precisely what the twenty-first century demands, and it is a philosophy and style (with an accompanying set of skills) that will work well in the new century.

FROM REACTIVE TO PROACTIVE MANAGEMENT

The Management Training School of Parenthood: Dumb Things Parents Do

Anyone who has graduated from the great Management Training School of Parenthood (raised a child successfully in the modern era) surely qualifies as a highly skilled manager who is capable of handling major stress and optimistic about the future. Successful parenting, almost by definition, requires the skilled use of positive and proactive problem-solving skills and infinite patience (no quick fixes here), but even the most successful parents typically learn their skills on the job. It is in no way contradictory that parents get smart, so to speak, after a period of dumb, and reactive, parenting. "Dumb" became fashionable for a period of time in the mid 1990s, a fad which rapidly gave way to the enduring recognition that smart behavior is much more adaptive in just about every respect, especially with regard to raising children.

Almost every successful parent has of course learned from dumb mistakes. So has just about every successful manager and organization. While dumb parental mistakes range from the humble to breathtaking, one of the more mundane but common parental goofs is putting too much food on the child's plate. The well-meaning parent, in his or her effort to raise a healthy and well-fed child and to be a good mom or dad, heaps the plate of the child high with food and says something like, "Now, son, you've got to eat your dinner in order to grow up to be big and strong and smart." The child, already smart and having been through this encounter innumerable times before, rapidly develops strategies to avoid dealing with the impossible: a plateful of far more food than he could ever possibly eat.

Well-meaning but wildly overreactive parenting produces predictable resistance. Number one son (first-born children are subjected to the overfilled-plate phenomenon more often than later-born children) at first says, "I can't eat it." When told he must eat it or face punishment, he resists by pecking away at an isolated pile of nonvegetable matter. This is often followed by a plea bargain: Can I eat just my potatoes? When these diversions fail, he may discreetly hide food under the table or the rug or find a sneaky way to feed the family dog. Most parents recognize these maneuvers: many can describe dozens of others. The most unseemly food fights, it seems, are between force-feeding parents and rebellious children.

While forcing children to eat is the bottom line for the overreactive parent, with all the negativity that accompanies authoritarian management, many parents eventually discover a much more proactive, and smarter, feeding technique: putting *too little* food on the kid's plate. This simple strategy may horrify the parent who is filled with guilt ("I'm a bad parent, starving my kid") but it is a wonderful strategy, because it works. The child eats her portion, and then if she wants more food, she *asks* for it. Theory X assumptions about children are more common than Theory X assumptions about employees: Just about every kid in the world is smart enough to ask for more food when she wants it and is grateful when she gets it. Feeding time becomes a pleasure and the child develops a positive attitude about food.

There is an exception to this technique, however, and that is the consumption of vegetables—the Waterloo of millions of parents. Kids love junk food and they hate vegetables. This is defective genetic behavior among humans, but it will never change nor will the defective gene causing it ever be discovered. Despite the ingrained hatred of children for vegetables, force-feeding is still not recommended. Some proactive parents have discovered that there are some vegetables that their offspring actually *like*. The same little monster who hides his peas under the plate in disgust actually gulps down his corn—well, eats his corn. The kid may end up eating corn five days a week, but the question that needs to be asked here is, "So what?"*

Positive parenting has become the subject of numerous articles and books in recent years. Children need love, guidance, and support, admittedly; but even more, they need a chance to make positive choices. Proactive parenting accomplishes this by creating choices that virtually any child can understand: "Frankie, if you will clean up your room this morning (well, the *corner* of the room) we can go to the zoo this afternoon." If the child resists, no zoo, but that is his choice. If the child does not stop throwing a temper tantrum, and now, then he can spend an hour alone in his room (quality time for the parent!). The choice is his. Discipline becomes proactive and much less punitive.

The analogy to managing problem people at work is, of course, irresistible. In many cases, the problem employee has an overactive child

---

* Parents sometimes go so berserk with happiness when the child eats corn that they proceed to heap the plate with big portions. No, no. Remember: *small* portions.

hiding within him, and the problem behavior—whatever it may be—may represent an unconscious cry for help from caring management. Initially, however, it is the problem *behavior* that proactive management must confront. If the employee has been coming in late, then he must make a pledge to begin coming in on time, or management will have no choice but to dock his pay or suspend him. The choice is the employee's.

Beneath problem behavior in the workplace we often find a big mess of human unhappiness. The myriad of human problems never ceases to amaze. The Employee Assistance Programs (EAPs) that sprang up in the 1980s and 1990s are a wonderful source of help for the manager who is not a professional therapist and who recognizes a problem that may require outside and long-term attention. The proactive manager is acting as a loving parent when he or she refers a problem employee to an assistance program or support group for help.

NINETEENTH-CENTURY-MANAGEMENT REVISITED

The Curses of the Vertical Organization: Mind-Sets and Meetings

It would be a simpler world if all the causes of reactive management, and its consequences, were based in the human psyche; but in the real world, with all its complexities, reactive management is also the result of the very way organizations are structured. The traditional vertical, hierarchical organization with its legions of functional specialists and formal managers carries within its compartments two curses of the human condition: mind-sets and meetings. Quite apart from their ability to depress even the most resilient and upbeat psyche, both often impose a major impediment to getting work done.

The development and uses of mind-sets in the vertical organization have already been discussed. Specialists or experts in functional areas are dependably competent in those areas, with occasional exceptions, but the price of excessive specialization is tunnel vision and rigidity, and vertical, highly functionalized corporations suffer from this affliction in abundance.

Specialization/functionalization often leads to an even more deadly ailment, however, and that is the paralysis and total organizational exhaustion that results from *excessive meetings*. The very word, meeting, in the traditional organization has come to have a variety of connotations, all of them derogatory and highly emotional: tedious and boring, waste of time, lengthy (or endless), irritating, and exhausting. Speaking of exhaustion, this list is by no means exhaustive. Meetings have come to have a bad name, and for a good reason. In a bureaucratized, hierarchical company, meetings are required not only to carry out the routine work of the various functional departments, but they are also necessary for the organization to coordinate such important activities as product development and planning. They are so frequent they seem to have a life of their own: Life at work becomes a series of meetings.

The curse of meetings is complicated and worsened by the fact that many planning and development meetings are carried on in *committees*, another word that has as many negative connotations as meetings. A committee in a hierarchical organization is simply any group that meets on a regular basis and hierarchical organizations have committees who meet in abundance. To the earlier list of connotations attached to meetings, the word "powerlessness" might be added with regard to committees. Committees may have meetings and make decisions, but the real power in the vertical company lies at the top: Major decisions are made at the top and then passed down to the troops.

Functional specialists from various functional departments eventu-ally develop a specialized outlook and values, and when they meet with specialists from other departments, good communication not only does not occur, but miscommunication and protection of departmental turf are almost inevitable. Not only does the left hand not know what the right hand is doing—the two hands do not even realize they are on the same body. Anyone in the organizational world who has ever attended a meeting where accountants, engineers, marketing people, and financial analysts have discussed the development of a new product can relate to this simple analogy with great feeling.

Since a product decision is normally of great strategic importance, unproductive and tiresome wrangling in a product committee meeting does not inspire executive confidence. The decisions made by such groups often suffer a similar fate: They do not make sense to senior managers who must take a broad and creative view of strategic decisions. Specialized mind-sets reach their level of incompetence at this organizational level, and the lack of productivity of various committees (complained about by all) is seen as a waste of the organization's energy.

An alternative to wasteful department-based meetings and conflict is a necessity in the twenty-first-century organization. The mechanisms that are emerging, and are discussed in detail in later chapters, are self-directed work teams, empowered work teams, and cross-functional groups. These groups meet regularly, as groups, but they do so with a singular purpose, and that is to get the creative work of the organization done.*

---

* One of the informal signs I look for in my consulting work that an organization is rigid and reactive is how often employees and managers are called away from training programs to attend meetings. In an overreactive organization they are called away for "emergencies."

TWENTY-FIRST-CENTURY MANAGEMENT IN ACTION

The American Defense Industry Changeth: Three Proactive Organizations

The American defense industry sailed through the early and mid 1980s, buoyed by record defense expenditures and the continuing menace of world communism, led by the aggressive Soviet Union with its formidable nuclear arsenal. Then a funny thing happened on the way to work: communism died. Historians may argue about exactly what led to the break-up of the Soviet Union and the outbreak of capitalism (or at least market economies) throughout the world, but there is already enough hindsight for at least one clear judgment to be made. Communism died because it was bureaucratic, reactive, and denied the customer choice. It was not in step with the emerging world.

The American defense industry, unfortunately, was nearly as reactive and out of step with change. Its basic mind-set was that the salad days would last forever and that the global market for military hardware would continue to boom. Reality disabused the industry of this notion, however, and a scramble began. Most firms opted to downsize dramatically (McDonnell Douglas, for example, laid off about half its workforce over a ten-year period) or merge (Lockheed and Martin Marietta were the biggest example) in an attempt to stay profitable while scrambling for dwindling defense contracts.

Other firms were true innovators, however, and displayed all of the characteristics of positive and proactive management as they attempted to turn around their organizations and position themselves to compete in the twenty-first century. In the words of Stephenie Overman, senior writer for *HRMagazine*, "Some forward-thinking companies have set up Alternative Use Committees to develop ideas for new products, such as solar-powered or electric cars, heavy-duty sport utility vehicles, or parts for high-speed trains. These committees rely on everyone from top managers to rank-and-file employees to come up with ideas. The goal: Everyone works together to create products for civilian markets that can be built side by side with defense products or, if necessary, replace them."[10]

AM General Corporation, based in South Bend, Indiana, went through a major crunch in the early 1990s, but the plant shutdowns and other crises it faced gave it an opportunity to get its labor relations in order and then develop new products. First the company negotiated a highly innovative contract with the Local 5 members of the United Auto Workers, which reduced twenty-nine pay levels to four, provided worker bonuses for productivity, and paved the way for worker-management cooperation. The company was in bankruptcy, but it decided to seize the opportunity to rebuild its four-wheel-drive Humvee vehicle used by the military in Operation Desert Storm and which had developed a certain popular appeal for the general consumer.

The Humvee faced some problems as a civilian vehicle, however. The company opted to use work teams to redesign it, and within five years had developed the Hummer, which could be used as an ambulance, fire truck, or rescue truck, in addition to recreational uses. Actor Arnold Schwarzenegger was one of the first consumers to buy a Hummer for recreational use, which pumped the company right up (bad pun intended).

Bath Iron Works, in Portland, Maine, has long been a shipbuilder for the defense industry, but it too has seen the light and is steaming ahead toward commercial building. While its future as a private builder is still very much open, it has already negotiated a highly innovative contract with Local 6 of the International Association of Machinists (IAM) that establishes a "teaming agreement" providing for joint labor-management committees with full decision-making authority in every functional department of the firm. Anachronistic work rules, which have plagued the shipbuilding industry for decades, have been eliminated and pay raises are now based on the willingness of workers to learn new skills—to become more versatile, competent, and multidisciplinary.

Bath Iron Works also recognizes that it must be market or customer driven. It is irresistible to remark that this is a company that has decided not to take a bath (yep, intended again). In any event, the IAM is also an organization that has recognized that it can no longer cling to past practices and attitudes, and it too has become aggressively proactive. Like many labor unions, the IAM has been faced with the need to create new jobs for its members, but it is unique in that it is developing a joint business plan with manufacturers on the West Coast to produce the Talgo 200 Pendular Train, a high-speed Spanish train that can safely travel out-of-repair tracks at speeds of up to 250 miles per hour. The machinists would manufacture parts for the new train.

While the venture is still in the early stages, David Clay, industrial projects administrator of the Washington State Machinists Council District Lodges 160 and 751, remarked that in such a cooperative effort, "there has to be an element of trust. Companies have to let us be aware of their business plan, their financial picture, their plans for new technology, so we can come up with a plan." Not surprisingly, he also notes that some of his union's members are ". . . stuck in the tar pit. They don't want to move. They only see our role as an adversarial one."[11] I cannot help but observe that the IAM is a labor union that is determined not to miss the train (three strikes and you're out).

The conversion of the American defense industry has also involved numerous closings of military bases, an agonizing process that has dramatized the worst characteristics of reactive and overreactive management. Each proposed closing has been greeted with howls of protest in the affected communities. Each base proposed for closure suddenly becomes the most important military installation in the history of the Republic, absolutely vital to our nation's security. The loss of jobs when the facility closes will be a deathblow to the surrounding community, according to every local political figure. The level of hysteria, and intense resistance, to each and every closing prompted the development of the Base Closure Commission, which creates a list of bases in each round of closings that Congress and the President must accept, or reject, in total. This proactive mechanism has expedited the process, but it is still painful.

What is interesting and instructive, of course, is what *actually* happens after an obsolete military facility is closed. In the short run there is indeed a negative impact on the affected community, primarily in the form of lost jobs. In the long run, after a period of from three to five years, new uses for the old base are found by the hustling and entrepreneurial members of the community, and the lost military jobs are replaced with civilian jobs, often with a net gain in employment (and income). The initial phase of reaction and denial, followed by hysterical overreaction, gives way to reality-based proactive planning, and the community emerges stronger as a result. It is hard to think of a better metaphor for the twenty-first century.

ENDNOTES

1. Developed and adapted from my business experience.

2. For a discussion of the role of neurotic fear in management, see Gareth Gardiner, *Tough-Minded Management: A Guide for Managers Who Are Too Nice for Their Own Good* (New York: Fawcett Columbine, 1993).

3. Timothy Nolan, Leonard Goodstein, and J. William Pfeiffer, *Plan or Die! 10 Keys to Organizational Success* (San Diego: Pfeiffer & Co., 1993) : 19.

4. Quoted in Lester A. Digman, *Strategic Management: Concepts, Decisions, Cases*, 2nd Edition (Homewood, Ill.: Irwin, 1990) : 22.

5. Jeffrey A. Timmons, *New Venture Creation*, 4th Edition (Homewood, Ill.: Irwin, 1994).

6. Robert Burns, "To A Mouse," quoted in John Bartlett (ed.), *Familiar Quotations*, 16th Edition (Boston: Little, Brown, 1992) : 361.

7. Rensis Likert, *The Human Organization: Its Management and Value* (New York: McGraw-Hill, 1967).

8. Donald M. Berwick, "Continuous Improvement as an Ideal in Health Care," *The New England Journal of Medicine*, January 5, 1989, p. 54.

9. Robert Gatewood, Robert Taylor, and O. C. Ferrell, *Management: Comprehension, Analysis, and Application* (Homewood, Ill.: The Austen Press, 1995): pp. 46–51

10. Stephenie Overman, "Efforts That Save Jobs," *HRMagazine*, April 1995, p. 47.

11. Overman, "Efforts That Save Jobs," p. 51.

4

GOOD-BYE BOSS! HELLO COACH! THE NEW ROLE OF THE MANAGER AND MANAGEMENT

Coach. Counselor. Facilitator. Project manager. Communication specialist. Team leader. Obstacle remover. Problem solver. Process owner. The managerial terms and titles are new, as are the roles of the twenty-first-century manager. Conspicuously absent from the new lexicon of management are terms like boss, supervisor, authority, and accounting/ engineering/financial/programming specialist, which we all associate with the traditional organization and the traditional role of the manager. The new terms define a new world of effective problem solving using proactive management skills.

The Customer Service Division, Sun Life of Canada (U.S.)

The Customer Service Division of Sun Life of Canada (U.S.), a heavy hitter in the insurance game, recently looked forward and saw a rapidly emerging reality: flatter and more flexible organizations. Based in Wellesley, Massachusetts, the division had long been organized into thirteen traditional functional groups such as sales, product development, and fulfillment, but it decided that the time had come to rethink its operation in order to provide customers with better service. With a "one-stop" service concept as its strategy, the division was reorganized into five groups, each with a distinct set of roles and responsibilities:

1. *Process owners* set overall performance targets and objectives for the division and bear ultimate responsibility for its performance.
2. *Process teams* manage day-to-day work and are responsible to process owners.
3. *Coaches* lead teams, help set team goals, are accountable to teams, and have responsibility for the quality of team projects.
4. *Product managers* are technical experts, but on product standards, and have the same responsibilities as coaches.
5. *Central support* is a support group responsible for maintaining functional expertise and for supporting and implementing systems development.

By getting rid of its traditional organization and focusing on key work processes, Sun Life of Canada (U.S.) has seen an improvement of 25 percent in on-time process performance and a 75 percent reduction in cycle times for major services.[1]

The sequence of managerial steps and skills the reorganized division followed closely parallels the Positive and Proactive Problem-Solving Process (PPPP) described in Chapter 3. First, all managers and especially process owners have responsibility for planning and strategizing:

Goal-setting and planning have been decentralized dramatically. Second, all managers (and their teams) are responsible for action planning and goal achievement. Third, implementation of goals and supporting systems is recognized; and fourth, the company is already evaluating the effectiveness of its new organizational concept.

General Electric Fanuc Automation North America, Inc.

General Electric (GE) Fanuc Automation North America, Inc., formed by a merger between GE and Fanuc Ltd. of Japan, is another company that has seen the future and understands that it does not include top-down management. The team concept that it introduced in its Charlottesville, Virginia, plant—dividing the plant into forty teams—contributed to record profitability for 1994 and earned the company recognition from the U.S. Department of Labor for outstanding leadership.

Both the planning and implementation of its reorganization are classic illustrations of positive and proactive management. The program was not implemented from the top down, which has been a cause of team failure in many organizations. Instead it was the result of a participative procedure involving a group of representatives from most of the functional areas in the firm: marketing, manufacturing, engineering, human resources, and the hourly workforce. Led by GE Fanuc CEO Robert Collins, the group met for more than six months to develop a plan to implement team-based management in the plant.

According to Brian Wilson, formerly a supervisor in the Charlottesville plant and now team developer of production operations, a number of plant employees were used to taking orders and interaction among employees was minimal. As a result, the transition to teams was frightening to many. The company made participation on work teams mandatory, but management's clear commitment to the program combined with a genuinely open communication policy was a big help in letting employees know this was not going to be just another "quick fix."

GE Fanuc's use of proactive meetings has been an important factor in making teams work. Teams meet weekly to evaluate their progress, set production and other goals, and design further training programs, and the entire plant workforce meets monthly to review operations (at one of these meetings one of Brian Wilson's teams was praised for developing a new cross-training program where workers rotate jobs every three weeks). GE Fanuc's skillful use of a proactive problem-solving process has raised the performance and productivity ceiling for a forward-looking firm.[2]

Living in the country that is the home of the quick fix and that invented the traveling snake-oil salesman we all might wish for a magic potion (sugar-sweet and swift!) that would take companies all the way from reactive to proactive management, overnight and painlessly. Alas, no such potion is available at the local pharmacy, even though dozens of management consultants continue to offer sure-cures to just about every organizational ailment in written form. What organizations like Sun Life of Canada (U.S.) and GE Fanuc Automation North America are discovering, however, is that a positive and proactive methodology for moving their organizations to problem-solving productivity works if given time and commitment (see page 106).

Four Ts of Organizational Commitment

At the organizational level, *commitment* over the long haul is absolutely essential for proactive techniques and a proactive culture and philosophy to take hold. Four Ts comprise the commitment process. The strong and continuing support of *top management*, the first T, specifically in the form of the CEO's verbal and behavioral support, is a virtual precondition for success. Even in our age of diminished respect for authority figures, the CEO and his or her executive team are still the major symbols of authority in the organization and are normally respected and admired by employees. When a newly appointed president and CEO like James A. Armour at AM General Corporation, manufacturer of the Humvee/Hummer, puts the full weight of his office behind restructuring his company's fractious and reactive labor-management relationship, good things are likely to follow. In the case of AM General, the company won an award from the Federal Mediation and Conciliation Service for effective use of problem-solving techniques in the bargaining process and developed a foundation of trust within the ranks of the company.[3]

In a society where CEOs are vulnerable to even short-term downturns in cash flow and earnings, he or she may take a significant risk in backing participative and proactive restructuring, especially when

---

The Four Ts of Organizational Commitment

• Management Support for Proactive Change

|

• Time for Proactive Techniques to Work

|

• Training In Multiple Competencies

|

Leading to

↓

• Trust and Loyalty Throughout the Organization

The Four Ls of Management-Skill Development

• Listening at Every Level of Management

|

• Letting Go of Authority and Power

|

• Learning Open Communications and Information Sharing

|

Leading to

↓

• Loyalty to and Trust in Management That Provides
  Personal Growth and Opportunity

Three Ps That Promote Positive
and Proactive Behavior

• Performance Appraisals by Teams and Empowered
  Individuals: Self-Administered and Empowered

|

• Praise for Genuine Accomplishment

|

Leading to

↓

• Proactivity and Positivity Throughout the Organization

---

it has been so well documented that during the implementation of these processes there may well be a lag in earnings. Yet CEOs like Robert Collins at GE Fanuc and division general manager at Sun Life of Canada (U.S.) Ian Kennedy have the courage to take that risk, undoubtedly with the knowledge that the turnaround strategy will succeed if given some time.

The role of the CEO as a visionary leader is particularly important during the change to proactive management. If he or she can develop and communicate a vision of change that members of the organization buy into and accept at every level, dramatic and transformational change can occur successfully. Dying companies can be saved and companies with flat earnings made more profitable. Lee Iacocca's highly publicized turnaround of the Chrysler Corporation (and he did it twice!) is the best-known historical example; current CEOs who seem likely to successfully pull off major transformations at Fortune 500 companies include Louis Gerstner at IBM, Arthur Martinez at Sears (after many fits and starts), and Gerald Greenwald at United Airlines (with the help of thousands of his employee owners).

In all these cases, the most cherished executive abilities are tested to their full extent: the CEO's vision of where the organization needs to go, his or her ability to articulate that vision to often cynical constituencies, and his or her ability to show leadership that generates the best kind of followership: trust and confidence in the head of the company.

A note of caution here: The role of the CEO as a visionary and charismatic leader in implementing change should not be confused with traditional, authoritarian, overreactive top-down implementation of radical restructuring (if the reader will forgive a real mouthful of jargon). The top-down model ("We're going to change this company, and now, because the situation is desperate, and because I said so") has all the appeal of a tough-guy quick fix because it promises immediate change, but it also has all of the numerous and very thorny obstacles of human resistance. Many a CEO has learned a lesson from the litany of failures of forced change (remember those airworthy computers?).

More power to CEOs like Robert Collins who join participative planning groups, listen to other members of the group, recognize the difficulties of the change process, and eventually get their entire organization behind them as they move to a more flexible and proactive management model. More power to them, and more power to all the employees of the company they empower right along with them.

Time Is of the Essence

There is no more hoary a cliché than "time heals all wounds," but in implementing proactive management, time—the second T—not only heals any psychic bruises that may result from changing roles and relationships—it also has the magical power of reducing fear and the resistance that results from fear. "Fear of change" is probably just about as hoary an expression as "time heals . . ." (the reader may well feel hoary-fied at this point), but it is also just as true. The change from reactive/overreactive management requires time for it to begin to work: at a minimum, one year.

To organizations teetering on the brink of bankruptcy, facing a crisis a day, time seems an all-too-precious commodity: far too precious to be wasted on planning a major restructuring and retraining program. Yet time must be allowed to develop a planning council, employee teams, and the other mechanisms that are necessary to bring about proactive change.

Time itself is no elixir, of course, but what happens over time is of great importance. When organizations use time to do proactive planning, to get groups of employees and managers from different functional departments or units talking to each other, and to begin dealing with the normal anxiety created by impending change, this time well spent typically accomplishes what it is meant to: a plan that will work because it can be implemented. The act of planning, and the fact of having a plan, even if it is imperfect and incomplete, is a major anxiety reducer in and of itself. A plan is something of an adult security blanket, but it is also a process and a product that stimulates us to think ahead and to be more proactive.

A final note on time and fear: it is an experiential reality for most of us that fear loses its power over time. The supervisor who repeatedly threatens an employee with firing may scare the wits out of him the first time, but by the twenty-fifth time the employee has become permanently deaf. Fear has lost its power to motivate him. The fear of change diminishes similarly, especially when a planning process is at work and that process is given six months to a year to take hold. Fear and negativity begin to give way to flexibility and creativity—healthy change.

Giving time for new-age, horizontal management is one reality; *training*—continuous, ongoing training in developing multiple competencies—is another. Training—the third T—typically occurs in two forms, on two levels: First, team members receive cross training in multiple job competencies, as is the case at GE Fanuc, where associates or team mem-

The Four Ts of Organizational Commitment

• Top Management Support for Proactive Change
|
• Time for Proactive Techniques to Work
|
• Training In Multiple Competencies
|
Leading to
↓
• Trust and Loyalty Throughout the Organization

bers rotate jobs every three weeks. Increasingly, both existing and new managers participate in the cross-training process, a practice that parallels what many Japanese firms have been doing for many years. In fact, Japanese practice is to cross-train an entire group of new managers in all of the work processes of a given plant or facility for a period of up to ten years before giving them a formal managerial title—usually as a group. An obvious purpose of such training is to build multiple competencies, but another is to increase group solidarity and bonding in keeping with the Asian emphasis on the role of the group in an effective organization.

Training in team management also is offered to both employees and managers emphasizing team-building skills such as goal setting, conflict management, supportive techniques, and self-evaluation. This type of training is absolutely necessary to give self-directed work teams a chance to work. W. Alan Randolph, a management consultant and professor of management at the University of Baltimore, comments eloquently on the importance of this issue:

When teams are created and called upon to make important management decisions, many otherwise skillful people are often at a loss as to how to function as part of a responsible, high-performing management team. (Several of my client firms) dealt with this issue by providing extensive team training. They taught team decision making, conflicts as positive phenomena, and team goal setting and self monitoring, as well as how teams could take responsibility for leading themselves. Over a year-long set of training experiences, coupled with on-the-job activities, individuals at these companies jelled into self-managed teams.[4]

Training at Randolph's client companies was not only extensive, but it lasted for an entire year.

It is a given in almost any organization and any type of work that empowered employees who are competent and who can make intelligent and independent decisions will be more productive. In the case that introduces Chapter 3, the team of construction workers who had been cross-trained in several different skills became so efficient that they beat the construction costs of established contractors by 100 percent. In most industries, competencies that cut across functional areas also lead to increased creativity.

One of the delightful realities of many twenty-first-century workplaces will be the power of highly competent people—who can build a house, or a car, or a clock from the ground up—to find new and better ways to design and build new products. Improved productivity in the manufacture of existing products is rapidly followed by greater creativity in new ventures. Confident, competent, and genuinely empowered people are a living example of good health: They take pride in themselves and their work, and they are powerfully motivated to continue expanding their competencies. Perhaps the most positive outcome of growth is that it leads to more growth and a lifetime of productivity. Just as untreated depression feeds upon itself and makes depression worse, good health and growth stimulates even more growth. It is a pleasure to face such a happy reality and such a positive and proactive self-fulfilling prophecy.

Trust: The Glue That Holds Together a Healthy Organization

Any civilized society is held together by the widely shared bond of *trust* among that society's members. Any nation's or neighborhood's sense of community is the result of that same bond. Trust is not an automatic outcome of living together, or working together, however. Trust among its citizens is the psychological outcome of a society that has learned to protect and nurture its members. Trust among the members of an organization is the result of exactly the same factors.

In an earlier book, I and my co-author O. C. Ferrell point out that we rely on the honesty and dependability of the people we are doing business with to the point that we take it for granted. Most business transactions are carried out with a handshake, or a nod of the head, because the parties trust each other. Violations of that trust, in the form of fraud or deceit, are so uncommon that they get our attention when they happen: We sit up and take notice and engage in the phenomenon that psychologists call *selective perception*. Millions of important social transactions, like baby-sitting, are carried out on exactly the same basis: legal contracts are not signed, but the contract of trust is binding.[5]

It is sad, but not surprising, to see someone like W. Alan Randolph state very matter of factly that "Bureaucratic organizations are typically close to bankruptcy in terms of trust. As a result, people exert enormous energy in trying to protect themselves."[6] In the bureaucratic, functional, and reactive organization, decisions are made in secrecy at the top of the organization, people and their competencies are devalued, employees live with unhealthy levels of fear, and the average or normal person ends up feeling that he or she is alone and vulnerable and needs to look out for himself or herself.

Major change in an organization cannot be implemented successfully without trust—the fourth T Period. Getting to trust is a challenge that must be faced in moving to proactive management, and the three Ts of organizational commitment that have been outlined in these pages are all important in building trust—and the loyalty that goes along with it.

The Four Ls of Management-Skill Development

When the four Ts are coupled with the four Ls of management-skill development, loyalty and trust—and high levels of personal commitment to achieving the goals of the organization—will surely follow.

At a company in the Midwest, where I was briefly a management consultant, a lonely suggestion box hung on the wall. While no one was ever seen hanging around the box, or even visiting it, graffiti would miraculously appear from time to time on its exterior. Many of the slogans that writers inscribed are unprintable on these pages but some may be repeated safely: "The Deaf Bin," "Home of the Heartless," and "Care Not, Share Not," for example. The president of the company, a functionally organized manufacturer of plastic compounds, would have the slogans washed off or scraped off by the janitorial staff.

Rarely was the interior of the box besmirched by a suggestion, but one day a terse note was found inside, which led to the death of the box. Employees joked, after the box was removed, that the CEO had the messenger killed. The note that did the deed read simply: "They put this godamned box up because no one listens to anyone around this godamned place, and this (common English expletive deleted) suggestion box is the surest (same expletive deleted) sign that (same expletive, plus company name, deleted) plastics doesn't give a shit about anyone. We might as well get rid of the (you get the idea) box." After the box was removed, the next joke (predictably enough) was that employees had finally succeeded in having a suggestion implemented.

Organizational graffiti, particularly the type found in washrooms, is one of the least used but most valid and honest indicators of the true state of morale in the organization. Suggestion boxes also serve as a lightning rod for discontent. The reaction of the CEO to the creative and heartfelt graffiti that it generated, unfortunately, was to blame the suggestion box. Is it safe to say that this was a reactive organization?

Is American industry changing? The 1994 winner of the Malcolm Baldrige National Quality Award, which was created by the U.S. Congress in 1987 to recognize quality improvement efforts by American companies, was Wainwright Industries of St. Peters, Missouri. Wainwright, which makes pressed and drawn metal parts for companies like General Motors and McDonnell Douglas, had an average of 54.7 ideas per employee implemented in 1994. The company implemented a Total Quality Management program several years ago, with accompanying changes such as quality circles, process-improvement teams, and a philosophy of continuous improvement and is now beginning to enjoy the fruits of a participative philosophy that recognizes the value of employee inputs.

In 1960 Toyota was a traditional, functionally organized manufacturing company with low employee involvement: Its suggestion program generated roughly 5,000 ideas per year, or about .02 per employee per year. By the mid-1980s, after more than two decades of process-improvement efforts, Toyota employees were producing more than 5,000 ideas a day, or about 50 per employee per year, and most were being implemented. The company, not coincidentally, had also become a world-class organization, with an enviable reputation for quality and productivity.

Companies like Wainwright and Toyota, unlike the anonymous but all-too-real plastics firm, have learned the power of listening, the first of the four Ls. They listen at every level of the organization, and then implement the ideas that result from good listening. If there is a single managerial skill that is readily available and easy for any manager to use, it is good listening. If there is a single skill that is difficult to implement in an organization, it is also good listening.

Good managerial listening requires that we overcome the traditional management mind-set that "I am the boss: I will talk, and you will listen." This mind-set associates good management with talking and telling. When we talk and tell, we are the expert, and we are in control. The twenty-first-century mind-set that a good part of good management is good listening reverses this perspective: When I listen I learn from all my colleagues and employees, and I have even more control because I also have their liking and respect. Changing the mind-set allows the skill to develop.

I consider listening so important to proactive management that you'll find an entire managerial- and personal-listening exercise and self-development program at the end of this chapter. Listening is the basis or foundation of just about every coaching and counseling skill: the coach listens first, then clarifies, or paraphrases, or asks a question.

Good listening is the basis of effective problem-solving in another way: It is a technique that a manager and team can use to brainstorm a problem, to develop literally dozens of potential solutions to the problem, and to come up with a plan that is practical and can be implemented in the organization. A major reason for failure in managerial decision making and organizational problem solving is the failure of decision-making individuals and groups to generate an adequate array of alternative possibilities and potential solutions to a given problem. Following the exercise and self-development program on listening you'll find a full description of the four steps that comprise a brainstorming session.

Brainstorming is a technique that builds on a basic fact of interpersonal and group life. In most decision-making situations, the minute an idea is proposed, the individuals or group involved begin discussing (and judging) it, and the entire decision-making session revolves around that one idea and no others. Committees, town meetings, and executive or board sessions are particularly susceptible to this phenomenon, but no group is immune. In proactive brainstorming, discussion is saved for later in order to generate as many ideas as possible.

Letting Go of Authority and Power

Good-bye boss! The phrase is symbolic, but the need is real. The twenty-first-century organization and its managers need to relinquish a good deal of the formal authority vested in them by a functional hierarchy and learn to use authority founded on collegiality and respect. Because this is no easy task, more efforts at restructuring fail because management (from the top of the firm to the bottom) is uneasy about what they see as power slipping from their hands in a "foolish experiment." Management hovers about work teams anxiously, watching for signs of failure, and then seizes the reins again the moment there is a downturn in production. Another self-fulfilling prophecy confirmed: "I knew this goofy self-directed team stuff would never work, and we need to get this organization under tight control again."

Alas and alack, and apocalypse now! The *real* letting go of hierarchical power—the second L—can be a gut wrench for a company

The Four Ls of Management-Skill Development

- Listening at Every Level of Management
  |
- Letting Go of Authority and Power
  |
- Learning Open Communications and Information Sharing
  |
  Leading to
  ↓
- Loyalty to and Trust in Management That Provides Personal Growth and Opportunity

because the traditional conception and use of power is so addictive. This is why it is clung to so fiercely. It is a very heady thing to be a senior vice president for operations or a chief financial officer. The perquisites of office, including many fine flights on the corporate jet, have great physical and psychic value, and the habitual deference of all those of lesser rank to a senior vice president becomes a routine expectation. Coaches, facilitators, and team leaders have no such formal aura of authority; indeed, the titles seem ever so slightly down-and-dirty. The coach is the fellow who screams encouragement and claps his hands as you slide into third base in a cloud of dust.

Three cheers for down-and-dirty and a cloud of dust. In the horizontal twenty-first-century organization, the titles change because the managerial roles change: The use of power changes from formal and legal to consensual.

Empowerment has become a buzz word, admittedly, and as such it can be simplistic and misleading. In part it means giving people the power to make decisions, but in larger measure it means freeing up the power of intelligent employees and their coaches and allowing that creative power to permeate the organization. Speaking to this issue, W. Alan Randolph remarks that ". . . empowerment is recognizing and releasing into the organization the power that people already have in their wealth of useful knowledge and internal motivation."[7] More power to the people means more power to the entire organization.

Learning Open Communications and Information Sharing

At the plastics company in the Midwest that owned the dysfunctional suggestion box there was an operations manager with a heart of gold. Unfortunately, his standard operating procedure was to work both day and night with his office door closed. His inner goodness was therefore not apparent to his subordinates, who complained to me about his lack of communicativeness and about the constantly closed door. They saw him as standoffish and aloof and gave him feedback about this one night in a devious but predictable way: They decorated the closed door with graffiti. "Behind a closed door there is a closed mind," read one slogan. "Caution: temperature behind this door below zero," wrote another creative author. The gremlins and goblins of the operations division had struck again.

After the appearance of the graffiti, and a heartfelt and honest conversation with me, the operations manager opened his door and left it open. He also began following my advice to get his butt out of the office and out on the floor, at least three or four times a day—to begin practicing Management by Wandering Around. I also encouraged him simply to talk—and listen—more with his employees, not only about production problems but about personal issues in their lives and his. The transformation was remarkable. One-on-one communication started and the graffiti stopped. The rest of the company remained rooted in hierarchy, but the operations division began to operate like a twenty-first-century organization, with people communicating and cooperating. "I should have done this years ago" was the division manager's rueful summary of the improved situation.

Open communications and information sharing is a process that simply must take place before an organization can become proactive. Executives need to share company goals, strategies, and financials; working managers need to share all the information that passes through them, both upward and downward; computer nerds (information-processing people) need to learn what sharing is; and employees need to share everything. Open doors in an organization are fine and necessary, as are open minds, but *open books* are just as important. Every person in the organization needs to know how the company is doing financially.

Learning open communications—L number three—seems simple and obvious enough, but developing it as a habit and a management skill requires overcoming the mind-set of power. Many of us have learned that by controlling information we can control people and maximize power, and nowhere in the organization is this more true than in data processing. The earlier, lighthearted reference to "computer nerds" had a purpose: Many computer-oriented people have learned all too well how much power they have as the result of their controlling information flow in an organization. Proactive companies have learned that the products of information technology must be made available to everyone, since shared information is shared power. This point need not be hammered flat, but it *does* need to be emphasized.

One of many reasons that major league baseball is in big trouble as an industry is the habitual secrecy and suspicion of both owners and players. Both sides make strategic moves in the dead of night, and the players believe the books are cooked—that the teams are simply not in as much financial trouble as they claim. It is safe to say that the only information that is freely shared by the bitterly divided owners and players union is performance data from the field: the pitching, batting, and fielding averages that every true fan loves. Lately, the precipitous drop in attendance and revenues has become information that the antagonistic sides in this best-loved of American sports have both been *forced* to share.

Loyalty and the
Twenty-First-Century Organization

The three Ls of management skill development lead to a fourth: loyalty. This is a form of loyalty that is both enlightened and new: It is loyalty that is contingent on the organization's ability to provide continuing opportunities for a person to grow, as opposed to unquestioning loyalty to the company, whatever it does. It is loyalty given now, but not forever. It is a loyalty based on self-interest and not on obedience. It is loyalty that will lead to the very highest levels of performance.

The competent, creative, entrepreneurial, and fundamentally self-interested person working for a twenty-first-century organization is a whole new psychological entity. The four Ts of organizational commitment and the four Ls of management skill development have a common purpose: to give such a twenty-first-century man or woman a chance to go on developing his or her creative abilities throughout a career. The demise of reactive organizations has led to the demise of the reactive employee: the simple and faithful person who assumed lifelong employment as long as she or he showed up faithfully for work and did the job.

The proactive mind-set of the twenty-first-century manager is more sophisticated. This manager asks, quite directly, "What does employment with this company have in it for me?" "Can I expand my skills while I am here?" "Can I expect fair treatment: to get back what I give to this organization?" The proactive mind-set is also strategic and action-oriented, and the new-age employee or manager will always be looking ahead and looking around. The opportunities that exist for the proactive man or woman in the new corporation are exciting indeed, as we shall see in Chapter 5.

Three Ps That Promote Proactivity: Performance Appraisals and Praise

Thirty years of industry experience with self-directed work teams, cross-functional work groups, and empowered individuals and entities of every sort has confirmed the wisdom of Rensis Likert, at the University of Michigan: Empowerment of any sort doesn't work if the performance appraisals and the administration of organizational rewards are left in the hands of functional managers. Reactive management is guaranteed when the reward structure remains hierarchical: Employees will work to please and appease the manager who holds the reins and the purse strings. The power of the purse is far and away the mightiest power a functional manager can have, and any good functional manager will use that power to promote and reward functional proficiency. Accounting managers typically reward accounting proficiency, and in this regard, accounting mangers are completely normal.

The performance-appraisal process can be a powerful P promoting proactivity and versatility in the horizontal organization. Virtually every company mentioned in the pages of this book understands this point: AT&T's Network Systems Division, which has reorganized the entire division around work processes, awards bonuses to employees if they earn excellent customer evaluations; AM General (a Hummer of a company) has introduced productivity bonuses for union workers; and the Eastman Chemical unit at Kodak, which has over one thousand self-directed work teams, has largely scrapped functional departments and now rewards teams for good performance.[8]

Functionally based performance appraisal administered from the top down is a major source of mistrust in the functional hierarchy. Two sorts of nonproductive, noncollaborative behaviors typically result in such a system, both of them more than slightly demeaning. When an employee knows that his fine manager, the head of the finance department, is responsible for his annual performance appraisal and salary increase, he will do everything in his power to *suck up* to his manager. Gifts, flattery, ass-kissing, and phony adulation are a big part of the behavioral package, and this whole set of manipulative behaviors is not lost upon other employees, who emulate it when they see that it works. Worse than sucking is *screwing*. Five finance department employees, who see all too clearly that only one will get a promotion and that Financial Fred will administer the promotion, *screw* each other in devious and creative ways. They backstab, sandbag, harass, criticize, and generally do their damnedest to make each other look bad.[9]

When sucking and screwing* are dominant behaviors in a bureaucratized hirerarchy, the competency and proactivity of the entire organization suffers, of course. Teamwork is a dream. Self-serving, cover-your-butt, turf-protecting behaviors are the norm. The classic Broadway play and movie *How to Succeed in Business Without Really Trying* is a virtual cookbook of how to suck and screw successfully in the traditional corporation. Since the traditional organization also values "nice" behavior highly, these terms are never used in the play, but the behavior of the protagonists demonstrates it beautifully.

More and more companies are solving the cooperation and proactivity problem by simply letting employees, both individually and in teams, appraise themselves, sometimes with management input, and sometimes without. The twenty-first-century mind-set in this regard is

---

* These are behaviors not taught at the Harvard Business School, but the eager student can earn a Ph.D. at the CYA School of Management, with a major in cover-your-butt and a minor in blame-the-other-guy. Please write to the author for application forms and admission criteria.

Three Ps That Promote Positive and Proactive Behavior

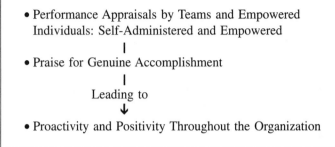

that no one knows better than the employee and the members of the team how well he or she is doing. Management's function in administering the appraisal process becomes one of helping set goals and criteria (in a self-directed work team, cooperation and collaboration are always important goals, and the performance appraisal process should reflect that fact). The performance-appraisal process and organizational rewards must be placed in the hands of teams and their facilitators. Teams of employees must be given real authority to make decisions about production, goals, and just about every other condition of their work lives. Letting go of power and learning to share everything have no more tangible and concrete expressions than letting employees and teams take responsibility for performance appraisals.

Praise is a second powerful P word in promoting positive, proactive, and problem-solving behavior. As managers, most of us are more critical, and less positive, than we think we are. Employee surveys are the best indicator: In dozens of organizations where I have worked as a consultant, managers have told me that they are surprised (and even stunned) by employee feedback about their management style. They see themselves as quick to praise and slow to criticize; the perception of their employees is the opposite. The managerial hurt feelings that result are treatable, often by a supportive statement as simple as "Your employees just need to hear you say something complimentary a little more often. Think of some genuine compliment you can give each of the men and women working for you, at least once a week." Most managers are quick to follow such advice.

There may well be 1,001 ways to reward and recognize employee achievement, but praise is the basis of about 1,000 of them. We usually think of praise as a verbal compliment, and most often it is, but praise takes many other forms: a gentle pat on the back for the man or woman who responds warmly to a physical expression of praise; a thank-you card to an employee who has gone out of her way to get a job done; a day at the ball park for the work team that has put in 15-hour days to finish a project on schedule; a small and spontaneous gift for a person who is putting in long hours somewhere in the middle of a project that seems endless. The creative twenty-first-century manager will think of dozens of such ways to give praise, quite on her own.

A final note on the use of praise: It must be genuine and timely. Real praise, of course, is distinct from the phony flattery given Financial Fred in the earlier example of sucking and screwing behavior. Most people who are being manipulated with flattery are bright enough to figure it out pretty quickly, and the price the flatterer pays is never to be trusted again.

Real praise, however, is chicken soup for the soul and a skill the twenty-first-century manager can put to use easily and with just a little practice. Like so many of the so-called "soft" management skills, praise works best precisely when it is put into use and becomes an important and often-used tool in the manager's tool box.

TWENTY-FIRST-CENTURY MANAGEMENT IN ACTION

Learning to Listen for Meaning and Feeling: A Managerial Exercise and Resource

The power of listening in good management is easy to demonstrate in a valuable, experiential exercise that virtually any manager can use. First, ask each member of the participating group to write down at least three or four of his or her significant or formative life experiences under the headings "happy" and "sad" on each side of a piece of paper divided by a vertical line. Each experience should be noted briefly, more as a reminder than a detailed recounting of the event. Encourage the participants to choose experiences that are meaningful to them, that helped shape or influence their lives, and that they feel they can share with a partner. You may also reassure them that this list of happy and sad experiences is a beginning list that can be added to at any time throughout the exercise.

If members of the participating group have difficulty in thinking of meaningful experiences, help things along by sharing a few of your own experiences, such as the birth of a child, death of a family member or beloved pet, graduation from college, or a marriage or divorce. Such sharing is an act of trust and openness and communicates to participants that sharing of personal experiences is okay. Your openness and honesty is a critical variable in the effectiveness of training and management, and this is a statement based not on dogma or theory but on my thirty years of experience as an educator, businessperson, and management consultant. Openness and honesty works just about every time.

Once the lists have been compiled ask the members of the group to pair off, with women talking to men as much as possible, and to sit face-to-face in as private a location as possible in the room. Explain that they will be sharing the contents of their lists of happy and sad experiences with their partner, with each taking turns as the talker and the listener.

Each talker has 5 minutes to share the contents of the list of experiences with the listening partner. Their communication goal is to share the list in enough detail that the partner will learn why those events were important. As they share their experiences, talkers may pause to gather thoughts, to reflect, and to add or delete information during the sharing process. The general rule is the more experience the better. Share what you can and share it generously!

Explain to the listeners that they must listen actively and attentively for the 5 minutes the talkers have to share their lists, without taking notes or interrupting. Encourage them to use positive body language and maintain eye contact with the talkers, to sit with arms open and not folded across their chests, and not to look away at the floor or ceiling. Let them know that at the end of the 5-minute talking period they will give the talkers feedback, so paying attention is important.

As the team leader, call out time at 1-minute intervals, and circulate around the room to coach both talkers and listeners: Watch for listeners who inadvertently or unconsciously display poor listening behavior or for talkers who seem anxious about a moment of silence ("Silence is okay—take your time to gather your thoughts and share with your

---

Eight Steps to Proactive Listening

1. Facilitator asks each person to list three or four *meaningful* (happy and sad) life experiences on a sheet of paper.

2. Facilitator divides the group into partners: men with women who are relative strangers, as far as possible.

3. One partner *talks* first for 5 minutes sharing his or her list of experiences. The other partner *listens*.

4. Partners switch roles and listeners give feedback to talkers for 2 minutes.

5. Partners switch again, and partners who listened first now share their list of experiences for 5 minutes.

6. Partners switch again for 2-minute feedback session.

7. Partners are free to have a *two-way* conversation for several minutes without active listening contraint.

8. Facilitator helps the group discuss exercise and debriefs session.

---

partner any of your experiences that will help her understand you better"). Most listeners and talkers rapidly become comfortable with and begin enjoying their roles.

At the end of the 5-minute period, ask the talkers to wrap up what they are saying, and then instruct the listeners on how to give feedback. "Listeners will now have a 2-minute talk, without interruption, and I'd like you to give feedback to your partners on the important things you've learned about them—the truly meaningful moments in their lives and how they've come across to you. You've listened to them for 5 minutes and now it's your turn to talk while they listen."

During the 2-minute feedback session, circulate and monitor listening behavior. At the session's end ask the group to reverse their roles, explaining that the entire group will discuss the meaning of the exercise at the end of the next session. When the second round of talking and listening and feedback session is completed, invite the pairs to have a two-way conversation about any unfinished topic that may have come up between them—or any other subject of mutual interest.

This phase of the listening normally leads to a major escalation of volume in the conversation and to intensified interest by the partners in each other. One of the most fascinating and refreshing outcomes of the process: That two relative strangers can become so intensely involved in each other's lives and interests in such a short time. It is rich fodder for the debriefing session—which is the final phase of the exercise.

The beauty of this exercise is that it demonstrates experientially the psychological basis of twenty-first-century management—trust. Other benefits that participants typically accrue include:

1. Understanding that an atmosphere or climate of trust, openness, and mutual warmth has developed between the partners. Some typical comments from participants: "I really discovered how much I like Joe and that this is the first time I've really gotten to know him." "This is such a good way to get to know a person." The genuineness, warmth, and humanity of this type of interaction is something that participants are most willing to talk about.

2. Appreciating that by listening to each other, they learn a great deal about each other—major events in lives, significant experiences, their common humanity. "It's amazing how much you can learn about someone when you just take the time to listen to them."

3. Understanding that listening is a skill that requires self-discipline. "I kept wanting to interrupt my partner and tell her that what she was telling me reminded me of my own experiences." The desire to interrupt is normal but must be contained in order not to interfere with the talker's stream of consciousness or flow of thought.

4. Learning that listening is a powerful way of helping. "As I talked about my divorce, I started thinking about it again, and that helped me deal with it." Active listening helps set in motion a powerful process of reflection, emotional understanding, or catharsis on the part of the person talking. We often think of helping someone as giving good advice, in the best tradition of Ann Landers, but active and empathic listening may be much more useful.

5. Realizing that listening is a powerful way of correcting or modifying the mind-set known as a first impression: the initial perception of, or judgment about, another person that we form or make upon first meeting that is almost instantaneous and that can be incredibly enduring. First impressions are often accurate and insightful but equally often prejudicial and just plain wrong: a projection of our own doubts and fears. "I found out that my impression of John, that he is arrogant and boastful, was way off base—I found out what a decent person he really is."

When we listen actively, we process not only the verbal information the other person is sending us, but we also pick up on a lot of the nonverbal: facial expressions, body language, and tone of voice. This entire package of information, coming through several communication channels, is extremely complex and rich and may correct a first impression based upon a single gesture, expression, or statement.

6. Understanding that listening requires that we give up power, or at least the illusion of power. When we talk at people, especially when we are giving orders, instructions, and commands, we have the feeling that we are in control. This is a subjective and often erroneous feeling. Managers high in need for power, who talk a lot, and listen only seldom, frequently produce the most powerful antagonism, and resistance, among their staff. When they need the cooperation and help of their employees most, such as in a complex team project, they are least likely to get it. Real managerial power, of course, lies in having the trust of others and the good will that goes with it. If this happens to sound like a short sermon from the mount, it is.

Good listening can be practiced proactively and daily simply by taking a few seconds to listen for both meaning and feeling when a significant other* in our lives indicates that he or she has something important to talk about. Research shows that the average American man or woman spends a surprisingly small amount of time with family

* A short list of significant others includes spouses, loved ones, children, co-workers, friends, pets, and plants. Pets and plants are unique because they thrive on being talked to lovingly, and this is easy for the average person.

members, co-workers, and friends: Estimates vary anywhere from 5 to 30 minutes a day. Quality time can be enhanced greatly by good listening.

A simple personal-development exercise that is also loving and generous is to use the listening skills discussed here for 30 seconds or so in an important relationship. The mind-set is fairly simple: "I need to put on my listening hat and pay attention to what Jane has to say—and to keep my mouth shut for an eternity of 30 seconds or so." Try it, you'll like it. And your relationships will improve.

The best relationships, including marriage, are between persons who are friends: who first and foremost like and respect each other. Adult love is an outgrowth of mutual liking, even though our theories of love do not deal with this proposition adequately, and there is no better way of expressing this than by giving a beloved partner or friend a few minutes of your precious time to indicate love and support. Listening skills can be practiced so unobtrusively and discreetly that no one but the listener may be consciously aware they are being actively put to use. This may be one of the most powerful messages of positive and proactive management: Its skills can be used effectively by just about any man or woman of normal intelligence who wants to put them to use.

TWENTY-FIRST-CENTURY MANAGEMENT IN ACTION

Proactive Team Brainstorming

Proactive team brainstorming is a technique that any work group can put to good use with little or no training, as long as it has a healthy appreciation for the power of good listening and can suspend judgment. In brainstorming, a team leader or facilitator poses a problem to a group ("What are some of the ways we can expedite the shipment of two key chemicals to our agricultural customers?") and then asks group members to think of possible solutions. A basic rule in all brainstorming activity is allowing everyone involved to have their say, while at the same time maintaining order.

Before the session begins, the team leader may say something like, "I'd like each of you to jot down an initial list of ideas for expediting shipments, without regard to their practicality. Write down any ideas you think of, and don't worry if they seem off the wall. Just think of any ways you can of expediting shipments." In proactive brainstorming, this technique is used to encourage the group to *suspend judgment* for a time and to begin a creative flow of ideas. Most team members have little difficulty in thinking of one or two ideas.

The team leader should recognize each team member individually, letting them state their ideas as clearly as they can without interruption. As members begin offering their ideas, the team leader writes them down on a legal pad or flip chart using a bold felt pen. A flip chart and a bright pen can be important practical stimulants for ideas because as the group generates a flow of ideas, it gets immediate feedback from the growing list on the chart. The team leader should also enforce a "no discussion" rule. No discussion means just that: As a member states his or her idea, the leader writes it down, but no discussion of the idea is permitted. "Discussion is something we normally think of as good," the team leader may say, "but in this first phase of brainstorming, it is bad. We'll have a chance to discuss ideas later. Right now, please *listen* carefully to each solution that is suggested."

Steps in Proactive Brainstorming

1. The team leader states a problem to be brainstormed and asks members of the group to think of possible solutions.
2. Group members share ideas verbally, *without discussion*, as the team leader recognizes them. The team leader records the ideas on a chart or board for 10 to 15 minutes.
3. The group discusses the list of ideas for about 15 minutes.
4. Each group member *rank orders* the best five ideas the group has produced.
5. The team leader *tabulates* rank-ordering data.
6. In the final phase, the team leader asks the group to finalize their choice for the *best* solution and best available *back-up* solution.

Within 10 to 15 minutes, a bright group will normally have generated anywhere from twenty to fifty potential solutions for the problem. The team leader will be kept busy writing! Two semi-exceptions to the "no discussion rule" may be permitted: Members may "add to someone else's idea, if it has stimulated a related or creative thought, and members may ask for clarification of another member's stated idea if they do not understand it. Each member should be encouraged to state an idea as clearly and succinctly as possible.

After the solution-generation session, the team leader asks the group to take another 15 minutes to discuss the list of recorded ideas in a freewheeling way and give them complete freedom to add and delete suggestions—to edit the flipchart—at any time. This session will be a rich and lively one, since the group's food-for-thought in the form of the posted ideas will be a very full plate indeed. The team leader should stress that no decision will be made during this period but that any and all ideas should be discussed fully and freely. The recorded ideas may be edited as needed on the flip chart.

Proactive brainstorming creates a specific product: a rank-ordered consensual list of solutions to the problem, along with a back-up plan. After the discussion period, the team leader asks each member of the group to spend a few minutes to create a numbered list of the five best ideas the group has produced, in order, starting with five as the best. Then the team leader collects the lists and records the points awarded each idea on a separate flip chart. The technique of assigning the five points facilitates tabulation and feedback. The best idea will accumulate the most points, of course, but the distribution of points is in itself informative: Is there one idea that is clearly best, or are there several competing for attention?

This rank-ordering technique is a variation of what is sometimes called the *nominal group* technique, but it might just as easily be called practical and proactive problem-solving. It is a structured, easy-to-use method that works because it requires full participation by every member of the group and every member's inputs are valued. Proactive brainstorming has a major advantage over other consensus-oriented decision-making techniques: It encourages consideration of contingencies. In the final phase of discussion, on a separate flip chart page, the team leader asks the group to spell out: What is our primary solution? What is our back-up, and when do we use the back-up if we have to?

Like many proactive skills, the six brainstorming steps are easy to master and very powerful when put into practice. If you feel somewhat tentative about using brainstorming in a group setting, a personal *mini-brainstorming* is recommended. In mini-brainstorming, after identifying a problem, simply list five or more potential solutions to the problem as they occur to you and put the list away for a day or two. When you take the list out, review it and add any additional solutions that may occur to you: then rank them in order of importance. Just the process of writing down more than one solution to a problem is an effective mind-opener and will get you into the habit of thinking in terms of alternatives and options.

TWENTY-FIRST-CENTURY MANAGEMENT IN ACTION

The Manager of the Future: A Portrait

A popular joke asks the question What do you call a person who speaks three languages? The answer, of course, is trilingual. Next question please. What do you call a person who speaks two languages? The answer: bilingual. And the final question: What do you call a person who speaks one language? Answer: An American. Groan or laugh, the joke makes a serious point: We Americans have a history of cultural and linguistic isolation and are having more than a little difficulty in adjusting to a world that has gone global and multilingual.

Closely related to the fact of an emerging world economy is a workplace and workforce that is more diverse—in terms of age, gender, cultural and ethnic background, and work ethic/attitude—than ever. Diversity will increase, not decrease, in the new century, which poses new challenges to managers in a new century.

Nation's Business considered these challenges in an article entitled "Nurturing Diversity" that treats diversity more as an opportunity than a threat. In a short captioned piece "The Manager of the Future," at the end of the article author Sharon Nelton interviewed experts regarding attributes and qualities of successful managers in this new workplace environment. The findings can be grouped into three broad categories:

1. Multicultural awareness and skills: Be multilingual, well-traveled, and comfortable in establishing friendships and relationships with members of other cultures—no more fortress America.

2. Education and literacy: Be well read, become comfortable with great literature and ethnic/minority issues. The renowned British philosopher Lord Bertrand Russell was known to complain in his lifetime that businesspeople were extremely boring because all they could talk about, or were interested in, was their business.

3. Be open-minded, fair, and ethical in dealing with employees. Ann Morrison, president of the California-based New Leaders Institute remarked that open-mindedness means "being willing to break from the past, being willing to do things that have never been done before, and to see people like you've never seen them before."[10]

And there's the rub. If there has been a single, overreaching psychological theme in these pages, it's that getting to open-minded is a continuing challenge for all of us but will be a pressing need for the twenty-first-century manager. Every single tip, exercise, mind-stretcher, and mind-teaser in this book has as its goal opening the shutters of the mind and making us more aware of habitual and normal mind-sets.

ENDNOTES

1. "After Re-engineering, What's Next?" *Supervisory Management*, May 1995, pp. 1–6.

2. "The Dream Team," *Supervisory Management*, May 1995, p. 10.

3. Stephenie Overman, "Efforts That Save Jobs," *HRMagazine*, April 1995, pp. 46–51.

4. W. Alan Randolph, "Navigating the Journey to Empowerment," *Organizational Dynamics*, Spring 1995, pp. 19–32.

5. O. C. Ferrell and Gareth Gardiner, *In Pursuit of Ethics* (Springfield, IL: Smith Collins, 1991).

6. Randolph, "Navigating the Journey to Empowerment," p. 22.

7. Randolph, p. 20.

8. John Byrne, "The Horizontal Corporation," *Business Week*, December 20, 1993, pp. 76–81.

9. Ferrell and Gardiner, *In Pursuit of Ethics*, p. 83.

10. Sharon Nelton, "Nurturing Diversity," *Nation's Business*, June 1995, pp. 25–27.

5

PROACTIVE OPPORTUNITIES IN A DIVERSE NEW WORKPLACE

Customer Driven a Given: Compaq Computer

Compaq Computer recently reorganized and downsized its salesforce in order to place its salespeople in closer contact with customers. All of the firm's sales offices were closed and each member of the salesforce was given a computer and told that henceforth they would be working out of their homes. All the computers were fully equipped, with networked access to databases containing complete and current information on company clients for the salespeople to tap into right up to the time they make a call.

Early results have been highly impressive. After two years of home-based calls, Compaq's revenues have doubled during a period of sharply falling unit prices. While the salesforce has been reduced to two thirds of its former size, productivity (measured in numbers of computers sold per salesperson) has increased by 600 percent.

Compaq's salespeople are free to schedule their own work days without permission from management. Internal demands on their time have been greatly reduced, with a major reduction in time spent in meetings, which has freed up a big chunk of their time and energy to spend with customers. Although the future seems bright, the sales force is now working longer and harder than it ever has before.[1]

An awful threat looms just over the horizon: a twenty-first-century workplace full of unpredictable, sometimes angry, people. The world of work and management as we have always known it has changed irreparably, and those good, solid, all-white, male, loyal, untroublesome, mostly middle-aged employees who once filled the ranks of the gainfully employed are rapidly becoming a minority, both among workers and management. What is the world coming to? To the twenty-first-century —and fast—is the flip answer. The more serious answer is that companies (and workforces everywhere) are coming to a much more diverse, globalized place where management faces new challenges and more opportunities than ever before. It is the opportunities that are the focus of this section of the book.

A Dynamic and Diverse New Workplace

The main facts of the matter are already well understood: White males are becoming a minority in the workplace as more women and members of ethnic minorities join the workforce. Women will comprise 50 percent of all new entrants into the workforce between now and 2005 and Hispanics, blacks, and other minorities will comprise another third. The workforce is also growing older as the American population ages—a trend that has been accelerated by a growing number of seniors who return to work part-time or full-time or seniors who delay retirement.[2]

The workforce is changing in another respect: With about 15 percent of the American labor force already organized into self-directed work teams, and with that percentage sure to increase throughout the early years of the new century, the ranks of middle management have taken a heavy hit. Managers will spend more and more of their time moving across a horizontal ladder, working with teams and individuals from other departments or units within the flatter organization. They will tend to be generalists rather then specialists, as Arno Penzias points out in a *Fortune* magazine article entitled "New Paths to Success." Such promotions will be the result of an individual's increased versatility and flexibility, coupled with multiple-task competencies developed on the same horizontal ladder. New employees will enter the labor force without the long-term expectations of the past.[3]

The number of full-time functional jobs will continue to decline, as more and more workers and managers enter the team environment, and this will result in companies' reliance on large numbers of temporary workers. Temps will be used both to perform functionally based jobs on a temporary basis as well as to carry out whole projects. A large percentage of temps will be women—currently, 72 percent of temps are women (and one third have college degrees)—enjoying the flexibility that temporary work gives them. They will also be workers with an attitude,* since most know full well that hundreds of companies are eager to have their services.[4]

Lastly, more and more employees will be working out of their homes, as the Compaq salesforce now does. Communications technology allows bright and computer-savvy employees to organize and direct their own employment with a minimum of help from management. Marketing and sales positions have always relied on a high degree of employee self-direction, but other jobs have similar potential. The busy corporate beehive, home to thousands of corporate drones, may not yet be completely obsolete, but it is likely to be downsized in the near future, just as the workforce has been.

How in the world does one work with such a motley crew? The proactive mind-set recognizes greater workplace diversity coupled with a new generation of worker attitudes as a tremendous opportunity. How do we organize and manage flexible work arrangements and a diverse workforce? Each change that has taken place in the workforce of the late twentieth century represents another opportunity to increase human productivity and creativity.

Every Employee an Entrepreneur

The most fundamental and enduring change in the workplace that twenty-first-century management will have to cope with may not be so much the restructuring of the workforce as the sea change in employee

---

* "I'm bright, motivated, and self-disciplined. Train me, treat me right, and leave me alone so I can get my work done. Thank you very much."

attitudes that has been a direct result of the transformation of organizations, particularly large corporations. The new attitude is an entrepreneurial one whose essence may be stated fairly simply: "I am a person temporarily under contract to you, and I will give you a good effort while I assess my opportunities with your organization."

While this attitude is arguably more prevalent among the young, who have watched the downsizing/reengineering phenomenon with often jaundiced eyes, older employees are modifying their traditional mind-set toward employers in response to the same changes. The traditional expectation of a new employee that he or she would be with a company for a long time, or for life, with opportunities for advancement and a complete benefits package has gone by the boards. Whatever the age group, however, a changed attitude is a response to a changed reality, which is that many new jobs *are* temporary and are advertised or described as such. Business professionals enjoying healthy contact with reality understand this and know exactly what they are getting into.

In an article in *Inc.* magazine entitled "A Nation of Owners," William Bridges calls this process "Dejobbing." Companies like Intel, Microsoft, Sun Microsystem, and Apple Computer have already left formal jobs behind, he says, in favor of highly flexible and loosely described "pieces of work" that fit into the larger pattern of what the organization is trying to achieve. This move away from traditional jobs and job descriptions has been extremely difficult for current workers to adapt to, Bridges notes, because of the traditional mind-set of what a job is.[5]

In contrast, the new wave of temporary workers has experienced this change in a much more positive way. The temp typically comes into an organization with no rigid preconceptions about what he or she will be doing and often cares less about a job title. She will simply ask, or be told, what needs to be done. The bright-eyed temp, who is often a very quick study indeed, also casts her eyes about to determine exactly what can be gained from this employer and the tasks he would like to have performed. One of my graduate students, who has worked several different temporary jobs over a period of three years, put it in a singularly refreshing way:

> "I loved those temp positions. You could learn something in every one. I learned so much in three years, especially about computers, you just wouldn't believe. Most of the companies were great—they were neat people who pretty much left me alone as soon as they figured out I knew what I was doing. Only one guy was a jerk—he bugged me all the time—so I just got up and walked out of there. All the others just about begged me to stay and I loved working for them. Now I work full time, and I make more money, but sometimes I get so bored."[6]

Training as a temp, interestingly, is in many ways training that helps break traditional mind-sets, expands competencies, and increases flexibility.

Bridges thinks that all workers should think of themselves as contingent employees, who are in business for themselves ". . . as the owner of 'You & Co.,' a microbusiness and company of one. You & Co. is, in fact, the twenty-first century's most important small-business enterprise."[7] The contingent-employee mind-set, like the attitude of my graduate student, encourages individuals to think more of themselves as entrepreneurs with a variety of skills to offer employers, including the ability to work constructively on project teams with individuals from a variety of backgrounds. Organizations thus become assemblages of talent that flex and change as marketplace conditions change as opposed to rigid and inflexible structures that offer career employment.

The management style most appropriate for all this, of course, is positive and proactive, with the accompanying mind-set that (in the words of the astute Greek philosopher Heraclitus) we never step in the same river twice. One of the most positive and exciting implications of the flatter and more entrepreneurial organization is that in a real sense every employee and manager comes to have a role in formulating and implementing strategy. One of the greatest lures of entrepreneurship for American men and women has always been the creative opportunity to set strategy: The small-business owner not only runs the show, but he or she must think proactively if the business is to survive and grow.

The success of companies like Toyota and Wainwright Industries is a powerful illustration of the value of using employee input in strategy formulation and implementation. This is not to suggest in any way that top management should abdicate its special responsibility for articulating an organizational mission and setting strategy; it is simply to affirm what smart and proactive top management already knows: There is a wealth of creative talent at every level in almost every organization.

The Softer Voice of Women in Management

As women have continued to pour into the workplace throughout the 1990s, the so-called glass ceiling has not so much been shattered as it has begun to disappear. This much-publicized but invisible barrier to the rise of women into the ranks of management, long considered to be largely the result of the mind-set of prejudiced and insecure white males bent on keeping management an all-male club, coupled with the very real need of working women to take time off to have and raise children, has now also been seen simply as a function of time.

Women have simply needed *time* to make inroads into middle and upper management, in the same way that men have in the past. Now that women have spent more time in the workplace they have expanded their capacity to network for new and higher-level jobs, taken advantage of training opportunities to expand capacities and skills, and have been a major force behind the development of programs like on-site day care and flexible working hours that have reduced the child-care burden for working mothers. The statistics show a steady growth in the number of women entering management at all levels.[8]

It is interesting that this surge is beginning at the very time that the traditional vertical management ladder is disappearing or at least losing a lot of rungs. Women are becoming managers at the very time that self-directed work teams are rapidly expanding their role in the global workforce and while employees everywhere are becoming more independent, entrepreneurial, and sometimes just plain ornery in outlook.

Until recently, however, women in management have felt heavy pressure to manage the way men did: to be tough, controlling, and overpowering. This is the thesis of *Swim with the Dolphins* by Connie Glaser and Barbara Steinberg Smalley, a book that also makes the sensible argument that in a male-dominated management environment, women had to conform to fit in: in other words, become more like men. These authors profile the careers of successful women in business to make the point that women can increasingly succeed by managing more like women.[9]

This managerial style (being a dolphin and not a shark) is less controlling and more caring, is both rational and intuitive, heavily emphasizes cooperation, welcomes new ideas, and delegates whenever possible. These are skills that *every* twenty-first-century manager who wishes to be successful will do well to emulate. Glaser and Smalley also stress the power and importance of nonverbal management skills like good listening, not smiling or giggling at inappropriate times (which perpetuates the stereotype of women as lightweights), and maintaining eye contact. The opportunity grows ever larger for dolphins in a workplace where there have long been too many sharks.

A cautionary note on supposed gender differences: The all-purpose disclaimer needs to be repeated here and strongly; namely, more research needs to be done. Much of the available evidence on differences between men and women as managers is anecdotal and observational at this point, but a flood of more carefully controlled research can be expected in the decades to come. Differences that seem intuitively valid and obvious, such as women being better listeners than men, may well be validated by such research, and some may not; but the proactive and open-minded mind-set that both sexes can benefit from as they watch any man or woman who is an excellent manager is "What can I learn from observing the skills of this woman as she manages people?"

Women as skilled managers are a problem only to men who have narrow and sexist stereotypes. She listens, but he sees weakness. She encourages a work group to reach consensus, and he sees indecisiveness, and so on. Similarly, skilled male managers are a problem to women with sexist male stereotypes. There are obviously very real differences between the sexes, but one of them is *not* that either sex is free of stereotypes of the other. One of the most positive outcomes of having a rich mixture of both men and women in managerial roles in the twenty-first-century will obviously be what each will learn from the other.

Overwork and the Burnout Epidemic

An overwork epidemic resulting from reengineering and downsizing is afflicting both managers and employees in the American workplace today. A virtual epidemic of articles is appearing in the industry media, which worked itself nearly to death covering the phenomenon. Such witticisms aside, the problem is very real and the symptoms of burnout have become all too familiar: exhaustion, depression, emotionality, and battle fatigue, resulting in sudden resignations, incidents of violence, and a surge in turnover among highly skilled people. Seventy-three percent of Fortune 500 executives polled by Opinion Research Corporation of Princeton, New Jersey, agreed with the statement that "the threat of experiencing burnout is greater today than it was twenty years ago."[10]

While the problem is occasionally labeled a crisis by the more anxious media, by-and-large an atmosphere of hysterical overreaction has not developed. Instead, most organizations (and analysts) take a more proactive stance and have recognized that overwork and burnout are problems that have to be dealt with to maintain the health of the company and its people. A sensible first step for most has been to identity the symptoms and then to get to work on the underlying causes— overwork resulting from undersizing.

Several managerial and organizational programs have proved to be effective:

1. *Paid furloughs and leaves for individuals and groups.* One of the most positive characteristics of self-directed work groups is precisely their ability to work: to work long hours, to work harmoniously and as a team, and to generate a high level of creative synergy. The downside of this has been exhaustion and collapse after a long period of creativity. Smart and successful organizations, like Boeing in the aerospace industry, which has made extensive use of project teams for decades, learned early that its hard-working and loyal team members needed a break—a paid break—for a month or more, at a beckoning tropical getaway like Hawaii, upon completion of a major project.

   Canadian psychologist Hans Selye made a major breakthrough in our understanding of stress (which includes the creative stress of hard work in a project team) when he developed the concept of the general adaptation syndrome, or GAS. Normal people respond to a high level of stress by increasing activity and arousal to a higher level. In other words, they respond by adapting positively and creatively—they elevate their game a notch, as great athletes sometimes do in moments of great crisis. The price they pay over the long haul, however, if the level of stress is not reduced, is collapse.[11]

When a distinguished educator like Neil Rudenstine, president of Harvard University, takes medical leave for exhaustion after years of working 80-hour seven-day weeks, and a highly respected executive like Drew Lewis, chairman of Union Pacific, takes leave for alcohol treatment and exhaustion after a similar work regimen, we are looking at high-profile cases of collapse after a long period of stress.[12] The appropriate short-term treatment is complete rest away from the workplace, and the appropriate long-term remedy is reduction of the stress level and the person's workload. This is a tough lifestyle change for hard-driving, workaholic executives who are virtually addicted to working 16-hour days. The fear of early death can be a powerful motivator for such persons, however.

2. *Rightsizing the organization.* After the international wave of downsizing and restructuring began to run its course, hundreds of companies recognized that they had gone too far, that they had shed themselves of some highly productive people, and that they were now dangerously understaffed. In many cases they had enjoyed a short-term boost in their bottom line but were wise enough to recognize that it couldn't last. Restaffing was often precipitated by the vocal bitching of remaining staffers, who responded to their predicament in a traditional and time-honored way: loud and persistent moaning and complaining. "The squeaking wheel gets the grease," the old saying goes, and millions of American managers and employees have been quick to recognize the wisdom of the timeless adage.

3. *Proactive recognition of the symptoms of burnout.* In the case that follows this chapter, "Brian the Burned-Out Electrical Worker," an alert manager notices some common symptoms of burnout and exhaustion in the behavior of a young team member who has been working long hours assembling electric motors for nearly two years. The case is based on a real experience in team assembly and illustrates how a skilled manager can effectively use positive problem-solving skills to resolve a problem of burnout before it becomes a crisis.

George Watson, the team leader, after recognizing a probable case of burnout, sets up a meeting with Brian Walters, the employee, and makes excellent use of a supportive coaching and counseling style, including good listening, to clarify the problem and develop an action plan to solve it. He is gentle with Brian but tough on the problem. The immediate decision, to train a co-worker so Brian can take some badly needed time off is made with the full participation and support of his work team. A contingency plan, transferring the employee to a less stressful work group, is implemented later.

When managers are the victims of burnout, the proactive problem-solving process is similar, but the process of managerial burnout may be even more insidious than in a case of employee burnout. In addition to such widely shared stressors as long hours and greatly expanded task responsibilities, team leaders and other managers in flatter organizations face a daunting challenge: continuing pressure from top management for high levels of performance, including high levels of productivity and profitability. Such pressure is not surprising, in view of the pressure executive teams are under in just about every industrialized society to make or keep their firms profitable, but it is likely to be compounded in organizations where executives are uneasy about or do not fully understand greater team and employee autonomy. This pressure will reach a peak when an anxious executive fails to see a quick turnaround of a troubled company by team-based management.

One of the emerging and little discussed ironies of the new workplace: supportive, participative, and facilitative managers in a new corporate era under heavy pressure from more senior management and feeling they have no one to turn to but themselves. There may well be no silver-bullet solution to such a dilemma, but the use of proactive communication and full sharing of problems, up, down, and sideways, will help.

Proactive Management of Conflict in the New Workplace

In the hierarchical organization, much of the human conflict experienced by employees is organizationally based; that is, it is generated by the structure of the organization itself. The conflict most often takes two forms:

One of the self-defeating reactions that occurs in a highly stressful, fear-filled work environment, as we have already noted, is neurotic avoidance, and the most self-defeating (indeed, the *mother* of all self-defeating) avoidance reactions is to clam up and say nothing about the stress we are under to co-workers, fellow managers, and high-level management. Clamming up will tend to lull others into believing we are okay, particularly if those others are not very sensitive to the body language of stress—irregular breathing, short temper, mood changes, and unusual clumsiness, to name just a few symptoms.

Sharing personal stress and discomfort contradicts another traditional self-defeating mind-set—that it is not okay to share personal problems and concerns with other members of the organization. So much for another traditional mind-set. The proactive mind-set of the new organization is to share *everything* and to build the best internal organizational support network possible under the circumstances. In flatter, more flexible companies, full sharing is a necessity simply to coordinate activities and get tasks done, but it can also be a powerful tool to reduce stress and burnout.

1. Conflicts between functional departments "protecting their turf," e.g., accounting fighting with engineering at an aerospace firm over the cost of some performance improvements in a new jet fighter.

2. Conflicts between individuals within functional departments over power and status, e.g., the undignified sucking and screwing behavior among members of a fictional finance department in Chapter 4 as they jockey for an anticipated promotion. Both types of conflict drain energy away from the productive work of the firm and are inherently destructive.

This pattern of conflict almost forces companies to handle it reactively, or by overreacting. When two "colleagues" in the same department sabotage each other subtly as they vie for a promotion they know only one will get, management has not much choice but to smooth it over or pretend it does not exist (reactive avoidance) or to pull out the full formal authority of management to suppress it (see the chart on overreactive management on page 158). Sadly, even after the precious promotion has been handed out, the conflict will linger because the promoted employee will feel she has won and the nonpromoted employee that she has lost.

"Don't get mad, get even," is the truism that has become famous because it so accurately describes the real, if unacknowledged, outcome of conflict. After the nonpromoted employee does her "nice guy" number and congratulates the promoted one, any savvy veteran of corporate wars knows full well that years of the most creative backbiting are sure to follow. The most venomous and abusive pattern of interpersonal hatred may endure for decades unless one employee or the other leaves the organization. Conflicts between functional departments take much the same form, and it is thus easy to understand why the word conflict has such a negative connotation in the traditional organization.

In the flatter organization, the pattern of conflict that is beginning to emerge takes a very different, often difficult, but much more creative form, which positive and proactive management can usually turn into a growth opportunity for the firm. This type of conflict is between spirited individuals and teams who disagree about how to get a project or task done and is therefore task- or project-based. It is essentially an argument

Proactive Versus Reactive/Overreactive Management of Conflict

Type of Management	Attitude Toward and Handling of Conflict	Typical Managerial Statements
Reactive	Negative: Conflict a Threat to Harmony • conflict is denied • disagreements smoothed over compulsively • manager goes to great lengths to avoid conflict • conformity a major value	"Let's all be nice and get along, boys and girls" "I don't see any disagreement here—we'll just muddle through"
Overreactive	Negative: Conflict a Threat to Organizational Authority • management suppresses conflict using formal authority • individuals attacked for expressing disagreement	"Keep your mouth shut, dumb ass, until you know what you're talking about" "There'll be no more arguing in this group—be quiet while I tell you what to do" "Stop the fighting, or I'll punish you both!"
Proactive	Positive: Conflict a Creative Challenge • conflict *task*-based, not organizationally based • disagreements about how to perform tasks can be used to improve productivity • proactive problem-solving skills needed to resolve conflict constructively	"Looks like we've agreed to disagree—let's see if we can work it out" "Let's all speak our minds here—the more points of view, the better" "I value everyone's inputs on this problem"

about how to be more productive, and it is both inevitable and potentially constructive. Conflict is inevitable because ethnically diverse men and women working together on a team responsible for making an entire product or carrying out a complex work process are bound to disagree about work methods, the best way to make the product, how the team should be organized, or about how they should cooperate and work together on the team.

Conflict is constructive because it can lead to a win-win solution. There are at least five basic rules of proactive conflict management:

1. Every member of the group has the right to express his or her point of view on the problem.

2. Members may disagree with each other but are not permitted to attack each other personally, e.g., "I disagree with your solution, and I'd like to propose a different one" is okay, but "Your proposal is the work of a fool with one eye and half a brain" is not.

3. Asking questions of each other to further understanding is desirable.

4. Everyone present is a partner in making a decision that affects us all.

5. Every point of view expressed needs to be evaluated against the long-term welfare of the company and particularly the needs of its customers.

The proactive managerial mind-set that is needed to resolve conflict creatively and constructively is, of course, open-mindedness. The rigid mind-set of "I am right, and you are wrong," discussed in Chapter 2, will either stifle or worsen conflict and any and all personal attacks that are permitted and not apologized for will lead to destructive behavior that lowers everyone's confidence and sense of self-worth. Any and all praise that is given to someone having the courage to express his or her ideas will facilitate full discussion, raise everyone's self-esteem, and help bring about a creative and productive solution to the problem that generated conflict in the first place.

Management by Knowing When the Hell to Leave People Alone

I have always wanted to develop a management theory or label that would result in an acronym so mindboggling that even an acronym-loving nation would rebel. The concept of Management by Knowing When the Hell to Leave People Alone* fills the bill nicely, although it is also a serious and highly relevant concept as we approach the twenty-first century. Knowing when to leave people alone is pertinent to several different types of employees and groups that are fairly easy to recognize: mature men and women, mature work groups, and bright temps.

As work teams mature they become more autonomous and independent and require less and less attention from management. Senior citizens are well-known for their ability to work independently and for a well-established work ethic. Temps have already been discussed: After an initial period of training many cheerfully perform their tasks without the benefit of managerial assistance. Entrepreneurial employees of every age

* MBKWTHTLPA, for the truly curious.

and from every background love independence and a chance to make empowered decisions about their task responsibilities. The sales force at Compaq Computer, a highly professional group, has responded with enthusiasm to a positive and proactive reorganization that has freed them from time-wasting controls and left them alone to get the job done. Many salespersons are prime candidates for MBKWTHTLPA.

This is not to imply for a moment that management is becoming simply a matter of benign neglect or staying away from employees as they get the job done. The notion of leaving people alone is intended just to dramatize an obvious but important point in the psychology of getting work done, and that is that good managerial judgment sometimes dictates that the smartest thing a good manager can do is leave an independent, well-trained individual or work group to do what they have been hired to do.

Leaving people alone does *not* mean no visits, no encouragement, no questioning, and closed communication channels. To the contrary, proactive managerial contacts are welcomed by almost any employee, within reason. The idea of backing off, but judiciously, may be a bit foreign to a high-energy, achievement-oriented man or woman who is convinced that more exposure to his or her managerial talents is just what every employee needs. The idea that less is sometimes better contradicts a basic philosophical American ethic, but a thoughtful analysis of the dynamics of the emerging workforce shows that management by knowing when to leave people alone is a bold new concept whose time may just have come.

Diversity and Synergy: The Goal of Every Organization

Men and women, young and old, black and white, Asian and Hispanic, permanent and temporary, and all in the workplace together: This is as succinct a portrait of the twenty-first-century workforce as any. A diverse group of human beings, obviously; managed (when necessary) by an equally diverse group of human beings. The opportunity that awaits the positive and proactive manager in working with such a wonderfully mixed bag of people is to go beyond the mere assimilation of diversity to the achievement of *synergy*: the productivity of such an assemblage of competencies, all working together, becoming much greater than the sum of the individual talents, or, more simply, the whole being greater than the sum of its parts.

TWENTY-FIRST-CENTURY MANAGEMENT IN ACTION

Making Diversity a Strength: Hallmark of Kansas City

Recently Hallmark, the Kansas City-based greeting card company, formalized what it had been doing informally in managing diversity for many years: It formed a Corporate Diversity Council. This group quickly established its role as more than corporate window dressing by publishing a "Business Rationale for Diversity," a document that links proactive management of diversity to sustaining competitive advantage in the marketplace. Like many large, forward-looking corporations—including Corning, Digital, Procter & Gamble, and Xerox—Hallmark has recognized that diversity management is not just an emerging reality but a major opportunity to remain competitive in the twenty-first century. It was also well aware of a 1994 study by the American Society for Training and Development (ASTD), which showed that 73 percent of businesses surveyed expected the workforce to become more diverse over the next three years, but only 15 percent of those businesses had any kind of formal policy in place to deal with issues of diversity.

Hallmark's rationale for diversity is clearly customer driven and links the work of the Corporate Diversity Council to providing products that will be successful in the global consumer marketplace that the company must compete in. The council has identified nine short-term programs that it will focus on in a three-year time frame, all of which will be measured and evaluated by employee surveys. The list of programs is a virtual "How to Do It" textbook in corporate diversity management:

1. Incorporate diversity training in all the company's management training programs.
2. Communicate company progress on diversity in its in-house publications.
3. Build executive commitment to all aspects of diversity.
4. Involve every employee in committing to diversity and its benefits.
5. Develop employee career planning, including goal setting.
6. Train managers in handling diversity.
7. Analyze human resource policies to ensure they support diversity—especially with regard to meaningful rewards.
8. Commit corporate resources to make diversity a priority.
9. Develop ongoing assessment of diversity initiatives and programs.

Mary Towse, Hallmark's Director of Corporate Diversity, believes that the company's diversity management strategy has pushed it to diversify and improve its workforce even further. "We are able to recruit the best and the brightest, and the emphasis on diversity allows for full utilization of human assets."[13] According to Towse, the need to assimilate a more diverse group of employees is followed by the utilization of human energy in more productive ways. The entire diversity effort has helped the company to become more sensitive to the consumer.

Proactive management of diversity begins with the mind-set that people are different—and that this is good. It has as its ethical basis respect for individual and cultural differences and the need to treat employees from every ethnic and cultural background fairly and honorably. It also recognizes that all employees deserve an opportunity to expand their skills and competencies through appropriate training and coaching. This is not affirmative action: It is simply twenty-first-century management in action—management that seizes an opportunity where others see only a threat and utilizes the potential that is inherent in diversity in creative and productive ways.

TWENTY-FIRST-CENTURY MANAGEMENT IN ACTION

Brian the Burned-Out Electrical Worker

The Midwestern Motor Company, an independent manufacturer of electric motors and components, makes several lines of small motors used to power toy cars, aircraft, trains, and other toys that it assembles for several toy manufacturers in North America and Europe. Two years ago the company restructured and downsized; its Wisconsin plant was divided into thirty-two self-directed work teams, although the workforce was roughly two thirds of its former size.

Brian Walters was a member of a seven-person team assembling small motors at the company's Wisconsin plant. He had been a member of his team since the company restructuring. The team went through an intensive one-month training period, which included a one-week team-building seminar given by a Chicago-based consulting firm, High Performance Associates, Inc. Then they began assembling the locomotive motor for a Swedish electric train manufacturer.

The motor was an immediate hit. The Swedish manufacturer, which enjoyed an enviable international reputation for the quality of its toys, put a dozen prototypes of the motor through their paces, and they all passed its stringent tests and specifications with ease. A major contract followed and George Watson's team was soon working 12-hour days, six days a week, to fill the Swedish orders.

The team was a happy, close-knit, and highly productive group and Brian Walters was one of its most productive members. Aged 28, happily married with two small children, and a hard worker, he never complained about his team's long hours, and in fact expressed great satisfaction with and pride in his overtime pay and productivity bonus, paid the previous Christmas. His team evaluated its own performance, and Brian's quarterly performance appraisals had been outstanding.

After a month into their work, however, George Watson had begun to notice changes in Brian's behavior. The always cheerful team player was noticeably grumpy more often than not, and one day he lashed out angrily at Jane Easton, another team member, when she accidentally dropped some motor components on the floor, which slowed the work of the group for a few minutes. Jane was on the verge of tears, but Brian quickly apologized and she was equally quick to forgive him. George made a written note of the incident as well as a mental note of two similar episodes where Brian had lost his temper with other members of the team.

George was also concerned that Brian's physical appearance had become visibly haggard, and that he was coming to work unshaven and sloppily dressed. But it was another incident of bad temper that persuaded him to intervene. Brian was working on an assembly task, using a very small screwdriver, when he suddenly flung the tool against the wall (as George walked up) and muttered loudly, "I'm Goddamned exhausted. I just can't keep my head straight anymore—Goddamn, I'm just tired all the time."

George waited for a minute, walked up to Brian and put his arm around the younger man's shoulders, and said gently, "I can see you're upset, Brian. Why don't you just knock off for an hour. Take a walk outside the plant or have a bite to eat, and then come down to my office for a while so we can talk. I'll have Jim cover for you. Would you mind doing that?" "Sure, George," Brian said, "I'm sorry I'm so upset."

An hour later Brian walked into George's office and closed the door behind him. The following conversation took place:

George: Brian, thanks for coming in. Grab a chair. How are you feeling now?

Brian: A lot calmer, thanks, George. I just went outside the plant for a walk, blew off a little steam, and had a bite of lunch. I want to apologize for blowing my stack and throwing the screwdriver. I wasn't mad at you or anyone on the team. I think you know that. I think the long hours are getting to me. I love my job, and Midwestern has been a great place to work, but the last month I've just felt tired all the time, and I haven't been able to fall asleep nights. Mary, my wife, says I've become a real night owl, prowling around the house at two and three o'clock in the morning. I've even been yelling at her and no one has supported me better than she has. She's worried that I'm having trouble sleeping and I feel tired all the time.

George: I can understand that. I know she loves you a lot, Brian, and we all care for you here. You've been such a good team member. What do you think has been making you so tired?

Brian: I'm not sure, but I think it's the job. I know I need to get in and see my doctor and have a checkup—it's been over a year—but I don't think there's anything wrong with me physically, and I'm not doing any drugs or alcohol. Oh, maybe I have a couple of beers Saturday with the team when we finally get out of the plant, but that's about it. But that's the problem, I just can't seem to get out of the plant. I'm here 50 to 60 hours every week with the team, and when I do go home, I'm still thinking about the job. This past month or so, it's really gotten to me. The job's gotten to be my whole life, all I think about or do.

George: Are you thinking about it all the time, and worrying?

Brian: Well, yeah. I worry about whether we're making the engine right, and I know we are. I worry if production is on schedule, and I know it is. I've even started worrying about whether or not the other folks on the team like me, and I know they're all my friends. I'm making real good money, and Mary and I don't have any money problems, but the job's just gotten to be my whole life—all I think about or do. I love it here, but the pressure is killing me. I think I may need a break or something, George.

George: I think I understand the pressure, Brian. You've been telling me a lot. When did you last take some time off? June, wasn't it?

Brian: Yeah, I took a couple of days off and went fishing. But then it was right back to the plant. I'm not complaining, because the motor has been a big moneymaker for us, and for me. But it's been nearly two years, and 60 hours or more every week. I think maybe I need a longer break. I've got three weeks of vacation I haven't used, but I don't want to let the team down and mess up production.

George: Have you talked with them about some time off?

Brian: No, not really. Do you think I should, George? Would it be okay? Who would replace me while I'm away?

George: I'm sure it would be okay. Why don't you talk with them? Would you be willing to train Danny or Julia for a few days before you take some time off?

Brian: Oh yeah, sure. They're both good workers. I just want to make sure it's okay with the team. I really need some time off. Can I talk with you again about the job?

George: Of course you can, Brian. I want you to do that.

Brian: Thanks for listening to me, George.

Soon after their conversation, Brian Walters took a three-week vacation at a fishing resort in northern Wisconsin. Shortly after his return, he talked with George Watson again about the possibility of transferring to a team making a model aircraft engine for a California manufacturer, which worked shorter hours than his team. But he wanted to discuss any possible move with the members of the team first. George assured him this would be fine and said that it was smart to think ahead and develop an alternative plan. Two months later, Brian transferred to the model aircraft team, with the approval of both teams.[14]

ENDNOTES

1. Arno Penzias, "New Paths to Success," *Fortune*, June 12, 1995, pp. 90-94.

2. Michele Galen, with Ann Therese, "White, Male, and Worried," *Business Week*, January 31, 1994, p. 51.

3. Penzias, "New Paths to Success."

4. William Turnley, "Managing Temporary Workers: A Permanent HRM Challenge," *Organizational Dynamics*, Autumn 1994, p. 46.

5. William Bridges, "A Nation of Owners," *Inc.*, May 16, 1995, pp. 89-91.

6. Personal communication to the author, June 28, 1995.

7. Bridges, "A Nation of Owners," p. 91.

8. See for example Russell Mitchell, with Michael Oneal, "Managing By Values: Is Levi Strauss' Approach Visionary—or Flaky?" *Business Week*, August 1, 1994, pp. 46-52.

9. Connie Glaser and Barbara Steinberg Smalley, *Swim with the Dolphins: How Women Can Succeed in Corporate America On Their Own Terms* (New York: Warner Books, 1995).

10. As reported by Sherwood Ross, "Workplace," *St. Louis Post-Dispatch*, June 12, 1995, p. 19BP.

11. Hans Selye, *The Stress of Life*, rev. ed. (New York: McGraw-Hill, 1976).

12. Ross, "Workplace."

13. Gary Toohey, "Diversity Management a Productive Strategy," *St. Louis Business Journal*, April 24–30, 1995, p. 27A.

14. Developed and adapted from my consulting experience.

6

PROACTIVE ETHICAL CHOICE AND TWENTY-FIRST-CENTURY MANAGEMENT

Levi Strauss & Company and a Value-Driven CEO

Levi Strauss & Company has for decades enjoyed an enviable international reputation, and massive cash flows, as a manufacturer of apparel—most notably its lines of blue-denim jeans, worn by millions of men, women, teenagers, and little kids the world over. In 1984, Robert D. Haas, a University of California at Berkeley graduate, valedictorian of the class of 1964, and a great-great-grandnephew of founder Levi Strauss, took over as company chairman and CEO. In a year he executed a $1.6 billion leveraged buyout, taking the company private, and concentrated 94 percent of the stock in the hands of the Haas family.

In the mid-1990s Bob Haas launched Levi Strauss on a bold and visionary value-driven strategy, designed to take the old family-owned firm straight into the twenty-first century. The CEO's strategy embodies empowerment and participative management, is called "Responsible Commercial Success" by the CEO, and is a direct outcome of his deeply held belief that a modern corporation must be ethical, profitable, and socially proactive: It should make the world a better place to live. A set of six "Aspirations" written by top management serves as an ethical decision-making guide for the company and has been plastered on walls just about everywhere in company offices.

The elements of the strategy all have a positive ring. Like Nike, Microsoft, and Federal Express, Levi Strauss values major decentralization of decision making, empowering employees to participate fully in the decisional process of the firm. Team-based management is being introduced in all twenty-seven U.S. plants. The firm has established a diversity council to promote diversity and empowerment as competitive tools. Chairman Haas extols the virtues of the company's open communications policy: "I think our values help address the problems because we get more two-way communication." It surveyed 6,000 of its employees for their input on running the company better and spent a year and twelve million dollars as two hundred key managers planned changes. Levi's also has a tradition of demanding the highest ethical standards from its manufacturers and suppliers.

The strategy has had mixed reviews to this point. The company closed a San Antonio pants factory, which cost 1,100 workers their jobs, and moved production to Costa Rica. The team concept has bogged down in several plants as team members have fought among themselves, even though turnaround times have dropped. The two weeks of training most members got, some of it in group dynamics, was apparently not enough. The firm has been slow to move into the casual wrinkle-free slacks market. Although top management is all white (seven men and one woman), 54 percent of company managers are women and 36 percent are minorities, far above national averages. Company director F. Warren Helman, a San Francisco banker, sums it up succinctly: "The challenge for Levi's is to be sure that decisions are not just 'nice' decisions, but decisions that are meant to enhance shareholder value."[1]

The plain and simple fact is that most American businesses, large and small, are honest and ethical and intend to stay that way. Levi Strauss is not an aberration. Like most adults in our society, most businesses know the difference between right and wrong; believe in such "motherhood and apple pie" values as honesty, fairness, and trustworthiness; and carry out the vast majority of their daily transactions in an open and above-board manner. In an increasingly globalized and customer-driven world economy, there is even more incentive for corporations to develop, or maintain, honest business practices, especially as they become more deeply involved in international commerce.

Honest and ethical behavior is pretty mundane, however, simply because it is so common and expected. It is the spectacular shenanigans that get our attention: Arbitrageur Michael Milken making hundreds of millions of dollars from illegal insider trading, after he had already made hundreds of millions of dollars legally by pioneering the development of

The "Aspirations" of Levi Strauss & Company

New Behaviors
Management must exemplify "directness, openness to indulgence, commitment to the success of others, and willingness to acknowledge our own contributions to problems."

Diversity
Levi's "values a diverse workforce (age, sex, ethnic group, etc.) at all levels of the organization. . . . Differing points of view will be sought; diversity will be valued and honestly rewarded, not suppressed."

Recognition
Levi's will "provide greater recognition—both financial and psychic—for individuals and teams that contribute to our success . . . those who create and innovate and those who continually support day-to-day business requirements."

Ethical Management Practices
Management should epitomize "the stated standards of ethical behavior. We must provide clarity about our expectations and must enforce these standards throughout the corporation."

Communication
Management must be "clear about company unity and individual goals and performance. People must know what is expected of them and receive timely, honest feedback. . . ."

Empowerment
Management must "increase the authority and responsibility of those closest to our products and customers. By actively pushing the responsibility, trust, and recognition into the organization, we can harness and release the capabilities of all our people."

corporate junk bonds; CEO William Aramony embezzling millions of dollars from the highly respected charity United Way and using the loot to support the most lavish of lifestyles; and figure skater Tonya Harding, in collusion with her former husband and several of his dim-witted friends, arranging to have competing skater Nancy Kerrigan wounded and disabled before a major national competition. The publicity surrounding each of these events is intense and brilliant, and short-term. When the media flurry subsides we are all too often left with the unanswered question: Why? Why did it happen? Understanding unethical and illegal behavior, as opposed to judging it, leads the way to understanding a complex subject like ethical choice and is well worth a bit of our attention.

Greed, Need, and an Unhealthy Dash of Desperation

Greed is an emotion that is so powerful that, coupled with opportunity, it can overwhelm individual morals or values. Insatiable greed has incredible short-term power to dominate behavior and to obliterate consideration of long-term consequences of illegal and unethical actions. It is a major motive in the machinations of both individuals and organizations. Ivan Boesky and Michael Milken, both born poor, were driven to continue piling up illegal millions, even though the eventual consequences were time in jail and ruined careers. Dow Corning, which discovered a huge and lucrative market among American women for its silicone breast implants, ignored or suppressed evidence uncovered by its researchers two decades earlier that the implants might be dangerous. The financial consequences have been ruinous. The Colombian drug lords, with no known ethical standards to begin with, built hugely-profitable organizations to service the American black market in illegal drugs, oblivious to the fact that their blood-spattered bodies would eventually decorate the pages of world tabloids. Their gory deaths have not deterred eager replacements from entering the industry, however.

The flip side of greed is desperation. When an individual organization has negative cash flow and faces bankruptcy, illegal or unethical actions may be taken to save a business. In a misbegotten entrepreneurial venture in St. Louis about 15 years ago, I opened a can't-miss, sure-fire restaurant* that promptly lost gobs and gobs of money. In desperation—and to help cash flow—I did not forward money withheld from employee paychecks to the IRS. This resulted in major fines and penalties, plus a threat to close the place down (the proverbial blessing in disguise!). I had lived by normal ethical standards prior to this misadventure, but the stress of having about two dozen creditors calling me daily and demanding payment led me to do things I would not have normally done. A positive and proactive career decision resulted from all this, of course: no more restaurants!

Many financially troubled organizations that are normally decent and upstanding and ethical will sometimes cut corners, engage in slash-and-burn employee layoffs, or resort to dubious marketing techniques in an attempt to turn things around. Several examples illustrate the point. Beech-Nut Nutrition Corporation, in desperate

---

* Every damned fool in the world wants to run a restaurant, it seems, and I was one such fool.

financial straits in the 1980s, knowingly bought a synthetic low-cost concentrate (with not a trace of apple in it!) to make its "100 percent pure apple juice." When the scheme came unglued, two senior Beech-Nut executives went to jail. Several major airlines faced with large losses attempted to roll back their frequent flyer programs, in the face of fierce customer resistance. The resulting brouhaha hardly helped their already-damaged reputations.

The general impact of severe financial losses is to force an organization, or an entire industry, into a self-defeating reactive or overreactive pattern (see page 180) which usually involves not only questionable business practices but also a good deal of MBCCP: hasty, desperate, and poorly considered strategic moves are made that further weaken the company. Currently the airline industry, which does not seem to learn from its mistakes and has a long history of cash-flow woes, continues to engage in an annual round of ticket-discounting that in the short-run may pump up earnings for the first carrier that announces its air-fare sale but in the long run damages the whole industry. The short-term self-interest of one carrier hurts the interests of all.

Proactive Ethics and Enlightened Self-Interest

Like Levi Strauss, the proactive organization approaches business ethics and the related field of social responsibility with a long-term perspective and a healthy measure of enlightened self-interest. In most cases, the company has a visionary CEO with strongly held values, a

Proactive Versus Reactive and Overreactive, Ethical Choices by Organizations

Ethical Pattern and Outlook	Reactive	Proactive	Overreactive
Organizational attitude and philosophy	Avoids or denies ethical problems until they become crises	Anticipates ethical problems and their consequences	Creates ethical problems by its business practices
Favorite saying about oil spills	"I don't see an oil spill."	"We can prevent any oil spills by re-routing the tankers."	"The damned oil spill is not our fault."
Level of responsibility	Denies responsibility for ethical problems: placates angry customers	Accepts full responsibility for ethical decisions and their consequences	Denies responsibility for ethical problems: aggressively blames others
Representative industries	Airlines, Petroleum, Breast protheses	Computer software, Banking	Guns/Weapons Major-league baseball
Attitude toward people	Employees not listened to: top-down decision making	Employees a vital asset: Often have ownership	Employees used and abused: Terrible labor relations
Historical practitioners	John D. "Stonewall" Rockefeller	Founders of IBM, Stonewall Jackson, Branch Rickey	All nineteenth-century robber barons, Richard "Stonewall" Nixon

deeply felt sense of mission, and a healthy ego that wants his or her life's work to matter: to have a positive impact on business and society, and (yes) to have a place in history. Bob Haas of Levi Strauss is apparently such a person, as was Thomas Watson Sr., of IBM, and Branch Rickey of the Brooklyn Dodgers, who single-handedly integrated major-league baseball. Ah yes, major league baseball could use Mr. Rickey now.

Critics often note that proactive, ethical companies usually enjoy the luxury of stability and profitability until adversity threatens, and then their standards change. IBM may be a case in point. When its well-publicized financial troubles began, its proud tradition of never making unwanted layoffs went by the boards as it restructured and downsized, pretty much like everyone else (but to the accompaniment of tremendous internal agonizing). Despite its troubles, IBM never lost sight of its long-term best interests, characteristic of corporations that are fundamentally healthy and forward looking. To my knowledge, IBM was never accused of shabby business practices while it was going through internal convulsions. It just focused on making the strategic moves that would allow it to survive and prosper again.

Cynics question whether Levi Strauss' admirable commitment to its corporate aspirations will survive a major downturn in earnings. Indeed, a half-billion dollar restructuring of its product-development and distribution system, designed to speed tardy delivery of merchandise to retailers, may take a heavy toll on employees in terms of relocation and layoffs. A company executive, commenting on this in *Business Week*, said: "An environment of uncertainty produces a lot of fear. It's easy to regress to old behaviors in a situation like that."[2] Stress truly tests values and ethics, but Levi Strauss has a virtually unmatched financial cushion to deal with such exigencies. The smart money (well, mine!) says that the company and its people will maintain high standards, provided there is continuing top-management support, the corporate culture is given time to fully assimilate its aspirations, there is continued training of both employees and mangers to maximize participation, and the company maintains the trust and loyalty of its workforce.

Proactive companies and their managers are by no means perfect, of course, but in general they have a realistic mind-set about what it takes to stay in business in the long run. They know they must be trustworthy, both in relation to internal and external customers and to other stakeholders in the organization, and they realize that their business practices must be both legal (the law normally defines minimally acceptable conduct) and ethical, but they also have an ability all too rare in our society: They take responsibility when things go wrong. When an ethical problem or a potential ethical problem arises they understand early in the game what the consequences will be if they avoid dealing with it—if they lie, stonewall,* or deny—and so they act accordingly. They do their best to solve the problem, and they don't fall into playing the blame game.

Taking Responsibility in the Teflon Society

After fifteen years of scholarly interest in the field of business ethics and a whole lifetime of fascination with the dynamics of human behavior, it is still amazing to me what a difficult psychological

---

* John D. Rockefeller invented the concept of stonewalling when he and his cohorts evaded questions or told the technical truth during the oil-cartel hearings of the late 1800s. His evasions may have hastened the breakup of the standard oil empire. Richard Nixon's stonewalling during the Watergate inquiry, coupled with ferocious attacks on his critics, may have forced his resignation as President. The original stonewall, Confederate General Thomas Jackson, earned the nickname for his courage in battle, but as a military leader he was a brilliant and proactive strategist who ran rings around his opposition. In the late twentieth century, not one member of this historical trio is remembered as a politically correct person.

challenge it is for millions of individual men and women and the companies they work for to take responsibility when they have made a mistake. It is far easier for them, it seems, to vigorously deny that they are at fault and try to pin the blame on someone else. It is this single quality, the acceptance of responsibility for problems and goofs, that most consistently distinguishes proactive managers and organizations from reactive and overreactive ones.

Denial of responsibility for mistakes and blaming of others has a garden variety of causes. For many it comes down to the often irrational feelings of guilt ("Oh God, I did a bad thing!") when they screw up, accompanied by very low self-esteem. Denial and blaming others reduces guilt in the short run and shores up self-respect but is destructive in the long run when those who are unfairly blamed find an opportunity to take their revenge.

In retrospect, it is a good bet that Dow Corning and the other breast-implant manufacturers wish they had pulled their products from the marketplace, proactively, at the first sign of trouble. The financial bath they have taken has been ruinous, and their initial stonewalling may have made their plight worse. Johnson & Johnson showed the way in this regard in the 1980s, under the leadership of CEO James Burke, when it immediately pulled its immensely profitable extra-strength Tylenol capsules from the marketplace after a homicidal maniac (who has never been caught) refilled some of the capsules with cyanide. Despite the advice of Wall Street gurus that the company would lose market share if it pulled the product, Burke went on national television to explain the firm's decision. Like any proactive organization, Johnson & Johnson also seized the opportunity to develop a whole new generation of tamper-proof containers to protect consumers from maniacs, which has made every consumer of over-the-counter medications safer.

Not all companies or industries are as proactive as Johnson & Johnson, however. The petroleum industry, in particular, is perpetually taken by surprise when another large tanker runs amok (and aground) and spills millions of gallons of oil into yet another ocean channel. Almost by instinct, or perhaps because of its culture and the huge liability and clean-up costs it will soon incur, the offending company reacts slowly to the mess, only grudgingly takes responsibility, and proceeds to put out a variety of mealy-mouthed statements designed to placate angry consumers and environmentalists. The gun industry is aggressively overreactive when it is attacked by critics: It isn't assault weapons that kill after all; it's the people using them who do. Such logic has failed to win majority support among the American public. It is not entirely coincidental that many companies in these industries are rigidly hierarchical and run from the top down: Their executives and managers still have the mind-set that they are the macho men of American industry.

The importance of taking responsibility for a problem or predicament, even if the situation is not entirely one's fault, cannot be stressed too strongly as the bedrock and foundation, and just about all of the superstructure, of the proactive twenty-first-century organization built on trust. Many of us who grow up in a "Teflon society" where accepting responsibility for just about anything is a behavior we have rarely seen have never experienced the tremendous ethical power of responsible leadership and management. In our book on ethical leadership, O. C. Ferrell and I made the following comments:

> Taking responsibility is a powerful act, psychologically and emotionally. It communicates all sorts of good and helpful things to those around you. It lets people know that you are human, that you are ethical and honest, and that you want to get the problem solved. . . . Taking responsibility does two additional things: It improves relationships among people who must work together to solve the problem, and it reduces anxiety in the entire organization. It helps create an environment where people can begin to give up defensive behaviors and begin to deal with problems in a more open and honest way.[3]

It is sad that millions of people, and the organizations they work for, who have never learned to stop playing the blame game have their relationships and their lives poisoned by mistrust. Ethical and supportive leadership and management can be an effective antidote to the toxic effects of overreaction and blaming.

Ethical Leadership and Supportive Behavior

Ethical leadership and the supportive behavior that is its key component may be defined very succinctly with a *do* and a *don't**: *Do* take responsibility, and *don't* blame the other guy. Stay calm when a

---

* I acknowledge that ethics is sometimes a preachy field.

mistake has been made by an employee or team member, and do not go berserk with rage. Angrily yelling at someone who has just goofed, "You damned fool, I just knew you would screw up again!" would *not* be an example of supportive behavior. Saying instead "I think there's a problem here and we need to talk about what we can do about it" might well result in a more proactive and productive conversation. Easy to think calm, you say, but hard to stay that way. True enough, but the more you practice the behavior, the easier it becomes.*

Aside from easing the burden of fear in the organization, supportive behavior opens the doors of creativity. The defensive mind-set "I need to cover my butt" gives way to more open and effective behavior. Fear forces people to close down mentally. If an impeccable and indisputable scholarly reference is required on this point, simply check in anytime with the survivors of a particularly brutal downsizing and you will have your reference, in spades. Supportive behavior can lead to the psychological salvation of an entire organization, although not overnight, of course.

The 1990s, arguably, have seen an increase in the incidence of supportive leadership, although the political arena continues to be a conspicuous exception. In industry, CEOs like Bob Haas are becoming more the rule than the exception and, as more and more organizations see the wisdom of responsible, proactive, and supportive behavior, ethical leadership will be one of the hallmarks of the new global corporation—a virtual contract between the organization and its employees.

* Ditto.

Contracts and Trust Among Consenting Adults: A New Form of Loyalty

"People mourn its passing: the longtime covenant between employee and employer. We remember fondly the days when IBM could offer lifetime employment," write Robert and Judith Waterman and Betsy Collard in a recent issue of *Harvard Business Review*.[4] While it is clear that the concept of the lifetime company employee is disappearing everywhere it is not equally obvious what is arising to replace it. These authors suggest that a new covenant is necessary between employer and employee in which both share responsibility for enhancing an individual's marketability, both inside and outside the company. Employees must accept a mind-set of continuous learning, and employers must offer opportunities for workers to constantly update and broaden their skills, even if this means that they become more self-reliant and leave the company. The Watermans and Collard refer to this as the development of a *career-resilient workforce*. Many of the companies pioneering career resilience are located in Silicon Valley and are on the cutting edge of change: Apple Computer, Sun Microsystems, Raychem Corporation, and 3Com Corporation.

This concept is fundamentally a contract based on trust between consenting adults involving a fair exchange of services: The employee gives his or her employer an honest effort and in return receives frequent training and a chance to broaden horizons by moving easily from a functional department to a project team, for example. The employer is no longer a parent with a child as a lifetime dependent who may become even more childish (and less marketable) over time. Parent-child bonding and loyalty is replaced by trust between adults who are enlightened enough to understand that they have a mutually beneficial interest, even if this is not always long-term.

The notion of a fair exchange of services leading to increased adaptability to the continuing onslaught of change is highly ethical from just about every point of view. And the exchange, if it is in fact fair, should lead to the greatest good for the greatest number, which will keep the famed Scottish utilitarian, John Stuart Mill, from turning in his grave.

Ethical is one thing, practical sometimes another, but in this case the ethical thing is not only practical—it seems logically necessary. If they are to function well, twenty-first-century organizations need flexible and better-trained employees. In the age of the more mobile workforce companies risk losing talented people who feel they can do better elsewhere. Companies need the flexibility to adjust the composition of the workforce without having paroxysms of guilt when employees are let go, and employees need a chance to explore career options proactively, without feeling they have failed in their duty to a beloved parent.

Proactive Communication and Organizational Honesty

The communications hallmark of the twenty-first-century corporation may well prove to be a flood of information, moving effortlessly up and down and sideways within the organization and easily back and forth between the organization and its customers. Completely open communications and information sharing are a simple matter of necessity if the proactive organization is to function efficiently. Top management teams must share data with everyone up and down the company—no corporate secrets here. Plain speaking in the finest Trumanesque tradition must become an executive habit—no mind-baffling corporate doublespeak to obfuscate the obvious.

For their part, managers will have to be flexible enough to learn the art of talking up, down, and sideways, and listening always, just to survive. Top management must be apprised of a project's or team's progress. Employees—co-workers, temps, associates, and team members— need to be counseled, coached, and facilitated. It will be an energizing and stressful role for the twenty-first-century manager, and compulsive introverts need not apply.

The necessity for openness and information sharing is easy enough to understand, but there is an inevitable and powerful corollary of organizational openness that is not quite as obvious, and that corollary is honesty. In the company with no secrets, deceit cannot easily be hidden. Every banana-republic dictator in the long history of bananas has understood this point clearly: Shackling the media immediately after the midnight military takeover makes it easier for the corrupt dictatorship that follows to operate in after-midnight secrecy.

Three global trends are sounding the death knell for the corrupt and autocratic organization that is steeped in secrecy. The first is the information revolution. The second is the customer-driven organization, which is here to stay. When customers are in the driver's seat they demand quality, service, and integrity; they will not long put up with a business that practices manipulation, arrogance, and secrecy. Major-league baseball is just discovering this fact, painfully, and may finally receive management worthy of its proud heritage. The third is an entrepreneurial revolution that continues to rage all over the planet. It is this development that will continue to drive the transformation of organizations and their management in the new century.

Entrepreneurship and Employee-Owned Businesses: A Vision of the Future

While entrepreneurship now flourishes in the former communist countries of Europe and Asia and attracts all sorts of good publicity, it shows no signs of slowing down in the mature capitalistic countries. Two relatively new categories of entrepreneurship are emerging that are the direct result of incompetent and reactive corporate management. The first is the host of small firms that have sprung to life in the 1990s to serve the needs of major corporations that have downsized and now must outsource for some essential services from entrepreneurial operations, some of them run by former employees.

The growth of outsourcing—which includes all services supplied to companies by other companies, including temporary employees—has been explosive in the decade from 1984 to 1994 and shows no signs of slowing down. *Business Week* reports that employment in business services or outsourcing doubled to 6.2 million jobs during those years and that a major motive for outsourcing was reducing costs. In 1994 American Airlines outsourced 550 ticket-agent jobs at small second-tier airports to employees of Johnson Controls, Inc., and other service firms, and terminated its full-time agents, who were earning up to $19 an hour plus benefits. The jobs farmed out to Johnson and the other contractors pay much less: $7 to $9 an hour, with inferior benefits.

While *Business Week* questions the ethics of the whole phenomenon, viewing it primarily as another cost-slashing technique used by large companies to take advantage of low-wage labor, it also notes that the smaller, more entrepreneurial companies are sometimes more efficient than the full-time employees or units they replace. MCN Corporation supplies data processing to Ford Motor Company and some two dozen other large firms, and its productivity—derived from its efficient use of seven mainframe computers—has resulted in significant labor savings for Ford and its other clients. The net effect on the economy, and on incomes, may well turn out to be positive, concludes *Business Week*, if other small firms match MCN's performance.[5]

It is fascinating that while Fortune 500 companies continue to shed jobs (nearly three million since 1985), thereby making themselves leaner and more flexible, they have contracted with entrepreneurial companies (lean and flexible by definition) that have sprung up to serve their resulting needs.

The second new category of entrepreneurship, perhaps even more interesting, is the wave of employee buyouts of businesses that are failing—buyouts that are motivated by the employees' desire to save their jobs and their communities. These buyouts go beyond the well-established Employee Stock Ownership Plans (ESOPs), which thousands of companies continue to offer their employees. They carry with them a transformational message: that a new generation of entrepreneurial employees will demand a larger voice in the management, and a big chunk of the ownership, of all American businesses. The current generation of buyouts has been motivated as much by desperation as by a proactive vision of the future, however.

In the airline industry, the employee takeover of United Airlines was the direct result of a high-cost carrier's descent into unsustainable and continuing losses in an industry that has come to be dominated by low-cost, no-frills carriers. TWA's buyout by its employees was accelerated by its impending bankruptcy, and the carrier continues to limp along, moving in and out of Chapter 11 bankruptcy protection as its lingering mountain of debt is renegotiated.

Smaller companies in small communities where they are major employers are attractive takeover targets for employees who want to keep their jobs and continue to live in a community where they have put down roots. The Spartan Printing Company is a case in point. When the employees bought the business, they agreed to take a fairly heavy hit in the form of decreased immediate earnings, but they also bet that with proactive, positive, and highly motivated management they could turn things around. While the jury is still out on the long-term success of many of these businesses, in the short run they exemplify the virtues and values of employee ownership: dedication, enthusiasm, teamwork, and cooperation, and a renewed sense of community in a nation that needs it. Could we ask for a more positive and proactive vision of the future?

TWENTY-FIRST-CENTURY MANAGEMENT IN ACTION

Spartan Printing: Employees Buy a Troubled Business to Save It (and Their Jobs)

In 1992 the employees of a comic-book printing plant located in the small town of Sparta, Illinois (population 4,853 in the 1990 U.S. census), faced a spartan choice: arrange for a buyout of the World Color Press printing plant built in 1948 or have the company close it down, as it had a similar plant in nearby Mount Vernon. With 950 employees, the plant was far and away Sparta's largest employer: Its closing would represent a major blow to the close-knit community located about 50 miles southeast of St. Louis. No comical matter, this: A choice had to be made, and fast.

The choice was to save the plant by buying it out. Kenneth Foushee, a seasoned printing executive from St. Louis, was brought in to become CEO and president, financing was arranged for a $29 million buyout, and Spartan Printing was born. The plant's employees, 700 of whom are members of the Graphic Communications Union or the Bindery Union, ended up owning 73 percent of a troubled business. Overhead had to be reduced immediately. "In order to hold on to business we had to cut down on operating costs," says Foushee. "We had to focus on things like equipment operation and manning. This shook out to mean that total compensation had to be reduced 20 percent."[6]

After implementing this initial round of cost cutting, Foushee and his eleven-member board (which includes five union members) began to consider some proactive strategic moves to turn the business around and make the plant profitable again. One of their first decisions was that the future lay not in printing comic books, a declining market, but in printing magazines on coated, or slick, paper. At this point, the company continues to print some comic books, including *Archie*, its oldest customer, but the bulk of the business is now the 160 different magazines it turns out for 39 different publishers, including the magazine that all children (and any adult with any child left at all) love, *MAD* magazine.

The move into the coated-magazine market has increased the company's revenues and profitability ($72 million in sales in fiscal 1994, $2 million in profits) but they have also required that Spartan Printing launch a $16 million expansion. Among other things, the company is adding a $6.5 million state-of-the-art M1000B press that prints slick paper at 2,000 feet per minute. The company has hired its own salesforce and installed an automated warehouse system with a capacity for 5 million magazines that can be shipped in entire carloads, which is a significant cost-saving factor in this industry.

CEO Foushee notes that the company must continue to improve productivity and maintain quality for its customers. The debt resulting from the buyout of the company will be retired in 1997, but union contracts come up for renewal in the same year. Commenting on the unusual management mix the company now has, Foushee says, "The methods for management are experimental to some extent. I don't know of another company with this sort of mix between management and unions combined with the job of running the company. We are feeling our way and learning as we go, and we all hope that we are learning to be better partners."[7]

Spartan Printing may be experimental to some extent, but it is a good bet that its proactive management style and philosophy, its employee ownership, and its strong sense of community and social responsibility will be a prototype for many firms in the twenty-first-century. It is a good bet that employee entrepreneurs, who see opportunities where others see only problems, will continue to buy out not only troubled businesses but thousands of corporations in hundreds of industries and that the flexible, fair, and flat management systems they proceed to put in place will allow their firms to compete efficiently and effectively in free world markets. It is a bet this author is willing to make: Do I have any takers?

TWENTY-FIRST-CENTURY MANAGEMENT RECONSIDERED

A Devil's Advocate View of the Emerging Organization: "If It Can Go Wrong . . ."

While the economic and human pressures, coupled with the information revolution, that have been documented throughout these pages would seem to make the emergence of the free, flat, fair, and flexible organization inevitable, it seems wise to pause for a moment to give the Devil his due. Despite empirical skeptics, like me, reports of the Devil's doings surface almost daily almost everywhere. The Devil makes people do things they wish they hadn't (the Devil seems to have an impulsive, short-term perspective)—things that are hedonistic and sexual, or at least involve big bucks, and things that seem foolish upon more mature and careful consideration.

In addition to the Devil, we must also give Edward Murphy, an American engineer, his due. Murphy is famous for his legacy, Murphy's Law: If something can go wrong, it will. In sober recognition of both these worthies, it might well be wise to ask the question "What forces or events are there that might block or prevent the widespread emergence of twenty-first-century organizations, as we have been describing them?" There are several possibilities.

1. The continuing need to wield power in the organization. Thomas Stewart, writing in a recent issue of *Fortune* magazine, argues that project managers are the middle-management wave of the future and that middle managers as we have known them traditionally will become extinct. After noting that old-fashioned middle managers are dinosaurs, he comments that a much more agile managerial mammal is evolving in the new organization, one more likely to live by his wits than by throwing his weight around; namely, the project manager. Learned persons, like William Dauphinais, a partner at Price Waterhouse, are quoted in support of his thesis that project management will boom in the next decade.

Then Stewart adds, devilishly, that "the dirty secret of flat organizations is that they still need authority defined as the ability to say 'Do it, damn it'—and no one has it."[8] He details some of the stresses that project managers suffer from as the result of job complexity and lack of formal or traditional authority. While the article is somewhat tongue-in-cheek (he also notes that the new generation of managers will have power from its expertise in management and growing reputations as good managers), he also raises a serious point about power.

Will the decentralization of power, and the giving up of power, lead to convulsive attempts to regain it? Will cash flow problems at an enlightened firm like Levi Strauss force it to revert to traditional hierarchy? Will the entire flat-organization concept flounder because people just plain need to know who is in charge in order to function? These are all good questions, given the lure of power and its continuing promise of a quick fix in a moment of desperation or crisis.

2. The big companies are just faking it, waiting for things to return to normal. In another, somewhat tongue-in-cheek article in *Entrepre-*

neur magazine entitled "The Pretenders," Jeannette Scollard argues that major American corporations, in an attempt to win back alienated employees, have invented what she calls "industrial relations doublespeak" (which includes terms like employee empowerment and teamwork) that is imitative of what smaller, entrepreneurial firms are already doing. One quote is particularly delightful:

> Teamwork is one thing we entrepreneurs don't need instructions on. We have practiced it from day one, when we struggled to pay our employees when we couldn't afford to pay ourselves. We learned then that people don't really work for us—we work for them. We've always known that Attila-the-Hun management styles succeed only with slave labor. Instead, our patron saint is Joe Paterno: Penn State's legendary football coach is the ultimate team builder.[9]

Scollard claims that corporate casual dress days are simply another attempt to imitate the genuinely relaxed atmosphere of entrepreneurial shops. She also mentions that the corporate "intrapreneurship" programs that were all the rage in the late '80s and early '90s have been a bust. The attempts of big companies to copy small ones, she says, will fail.

True or not true? Scollard's article is provocative, but it overlooks one important point: that even the biggest companies are breaking down into smaller, more entrepreneurial units that tend to be loosely coordinated by an executive team. It is a good bet that big organizations are not just imitating smaller ones: they are transforming themselves—because they have to.

3. Proactive, participative management, and the concept of the flat organization, is just another management fad that will disappear as quickly as other such fads. Several million unused and forgotten hula hoops hang on pegs in American garages or lie hidden away in attics. We are the nation of fads and quick fixes, and we are well advised to be cautious, and skeptical, when a new methodology or technique is promoted as the sure-fire cure for what ails us, managerally speaking. Is proactive, participative management just another quick fix?

The quick answer is no, and the longer-term answer is also no. The basic concepts of participation and empowerment have been around for over three decades and during that period of time hundreds of companies have implemented participative concepts. The evidence that has accumulated strongly supports the conclusion that participative management is precisely *not* a quick fix to a company's problems and that it requires a good deal of time to work, even if given strong top-management support.

Does participative management work? If market valuations of a company's stock are a valid indicator, then a study commissioned by the California Public Employees' Retirement System (CalPERS) and released in 1994 strongly suggests that the answer is yes. The study done for CalPERS by Gordon Group, Inc., showed that companies that employ participative decision-making techniques consistently outpace companies that don't in the stock markets.[10] CalPERS is using the results of its study to target future investments. Proactive management appears to be an idea whose time has come.

4. A cataclysm such as a nuclear holocaust or a population explosion that will swamp the planet will cause a regression to traditional or primitive forms of organization. Ah yes, the apocalypse may well be upon us, particularly in the form of uncontrolled global population growth, coupled with the poverty and illiteracy it is sure to breed. A nuclear holocaust seems less likely in the twenty-first century than in the twentieth. Who knows, however, what humongous asteroids are lurking out there in space, waiting to crash into our undefended planet, wreaking unspeakable havoc.

The doomsayers should be given their due, but the human race has a long history of adaptability and coping with major challenges and so does the American nation. Yet Pogo's words continue to ring in our ears: "We have met the enemy, and it is us." Doomsayers and apocalyptic theorists were reportedly reassured when the baseball "World Series" (which may shortly become a truly global championship of baseball) was held as scheduled in the fall of 1995.

ENDNOTES

1. Russell Mitchell, with Michael Oneal, "Managing by Values: Is Levi Strauss' Approach Visionary—or Flaky?" *Business Week*, August 1, 1994, pp. 46–52.

2. Mitchell, with Oneal, "Managing by Values: Is Levi Strauss' Approach Visionary—or Flaky?" p.49.

3. O. C. Ferrell and Gareth Gardiner, *In Pursuit of Ethics* (Springfield, IL: Smith Collins, 1991): 69.

4. Robert H. Waterman Jr., Judith A. Waterman, and Betsy A. Collard, "Toward a Career-Resilient Workforce," *Harvard Business Review* (July–August, 1994): 87–95.

5. Aaron Bernstein, with Wendy Zellner, "Outsourced and Out of Luck," *Business Week*, July 17, 1995, pp. 60–61.

6. Robert Sanford, "Spartan Teamwork Puts Town, Plant on Printing Map," *St. Louis Post-Dispatch*, May 29, 1995, p. 9BP.

7. Sanford, "Spartan Teamwork Puts Town, Plant on Printing Map," p. 9BP.

8. Thomas A. Stewart, "The Corporate Jungle Spawns a New Species: The Project Manager." *Fortune*, July 10, 1995, p. 180.

9. Jeannette R. Scollard, "The Pretenders," *Entrepreneur*, May 1995, p. 256.

10. Mitchell, with Oneal, p. 47.

INDEX

Index